Symbol

LAURENCE KING

Published in 2011 by
Laurence King Publishing Ltd
361–373 City Road
London EC1V 1LR
United Kingdom
Tel: +44 20 7841 6900
Fax: +44 20 7841 6910
e-mail: enquiries@laurenceking.com
www.laurenceking.com

A catalogue record for this book is
available from the British Library.

ISBN 978 1 85669 727 9

Art direction and cover design by
Angus Hyland

Book design by & SMITH
www.andsmithdesign.com

Senior editor: Susie May
Picture researcher: Ida Riveros
Production: Simon Walsh

Printed in China

Symbol

Angus Hyland and Steven Bateman

Laurence King Publishing

Preface

As a child I used to love leafing through the *Encyclopaedia Britannica*. This was not symptomatic of a thirst for knowledge on my part so much as an instinctive interest in lateral thinking. What had me hooked was the manner in which the entries appeared: bizarre juxtapositions and marriages of subject matter, all arranged by the superimposed and seemingly arbitrary framework of alphabetical order. Such enjoyment may partly have been a result of my short attention span, of course, but the presentation of such diverse entries cheek by jowl did open up new and unexpected pathways of appreciation and absorption of information.

The idea behind this book is to explore the visual language of symbols according to its most basic element: form. We have brought together symbols conceived all over the world, in different times and for different purposes, and categorized them by visual type. Here they are laid out for view divested of all the agendas, meanings and messages that might be associated with them in their own customary contexts. Arranged in this way, the symbols are essentially isolated so that the effectiveness of their composition and impact can be assessed without distraction and so that the reader can enjoy them as a pictorial language in their own right.

Angus Hyland

CONTENTS

1

ABSTRACT

2

REPRESENTATIONAL

What is in this book

The symbols selected for this book naturally
reflect the editorial tendencies of its authors.
However, we were also constrained by the
fact that some corporations couldn't give us
permission to publish their corporate symbols
independently of their logotype and, as a
result, readers may notice some significant
omissions. *Symbol* may not be 100 per cent
definitive but considering the red tape
involved in brand security it's about as close
as you can get. Those interested in the
subject will find a whole world of websites
and blogs dedicated to this area of design.
Symbol nonetheless encompasses a vast
scope of work past and present, and we
are grateful to the many designers and
corporations whose contributions made
this book possible.

The captions

The caption for each symbol identifies
the client company or organization (in bold),
the country of its headquarters, the designer
or design firm responsible and the date
of design.

See how you feel

David Gibbs

'Symbol' is a colossal word. In religion, literature and art, symbolism has engrossed and fascinated thinkers and believers, writers and artists down the ages. One of the great games of civilization is the creation of symbols, their concealment, uncovering, interpretation and study. The way in which the graphic symbols in this book also lend themselves to these subtle games is what makes the subject so entertaining.

Changing meanings

What is meant by the word 'symbol' here needs some defining. This presents problems, because the definition has changed over the last century and continues to do so. One reason for this is the lax and relatively recent interchangeability of the terms 'symbol' and 'logo', which has been and still is confusing. Design is a business where the latest buzzwords can be embraced without too much thought being given to the consequences. So it was with 'logo' when it first entered the language in the 1930s as a cute and fashionable short form of 'logotype'.

Logotype stems from the Greek *logos*, meaning word, and relates to any typographic styling of a name or word that makes it easily recognizable or significant as a mark of ownership or identity. But if 'logo' once meant the same as 'logotype', it no longer does. It has departed from being a clone of its parent and come to mean a more general mark of identity. For some, a logo no longer even has to involve a word or words. For others, add a logotype to a symbol and get a logo. But that is a kind of post hoc rationalization of the confusion.

This modern use of 'logo' has pushed the meaning of the 'symbol' into a corner. Once the idea of a graphic symbol was simple: it was an all-embracing term for any single coherent visual device that denoted identity, recognition, ownership or affiliation. But now that 'logo' has taken up much of this space, 'symbol' has had to make room for it and confine its meaning to only those abstract or pictorial graphic devices that represent the essence of identity. This simpler definition has had the effect of refining the subject of graphic symbols, giving it a new and distinct status within identity design.

At one time or another, designers have also appropriated other words for use in the modern business of graphic visual identity, probably for no better reason than that they seemed to be fresh and appealing alternatives to the status quo and were taken up in much the same spirit that 'logo' was. 'Crest', 'badge', 'seal' and 'emblem' come from particular areas of identity such as heraldry, correspondence and engraving; they could also just be called symbols. Likewise, 'signature', 'totem' and 'icon' are names for symbols that first qualified in other spheres, from personal identity to religion.

There are also words that are technical and thus legitimately describe types of symbol. As such, 'monogram', 'logogram' and 'pictogram' are particular and explain and define themselves. Then there are systematized craft symbols such as 'hallmarks' and symbols used as 'trademarks' or 'brandmarks', which are vested with a certain kind of emotional appeal and power. 'Mark' has become popular as a useful catch-all. So a look back over the story of symbol design is best placed in this context of multiple and changing definitions.

Writing and trading

The family of graphic marks that are symbolic in part or in whole was once large. Symbols represent ideas and information, objects and feelings. The alphabet is a system of visual symbols used to denote language. As Eric Gill admonished: 'Letters are not pictures but signs for sounds.'[1] If language is phonetic, writing was originally simply a means of recording it or conveying it to people out of earshot, or for the record. But writing also then became a primary expression in itself, extending the spoken language into the written language – the phonetic into the graphic.

The use of symbols in trade and commerce goes back to the origins of market society. In the ancient world, makers' marks (*tituli picti*) were stamped or painted on the necks of amphorae used to transport wine or oil. Roman brick makers and soap makers were obliged to mark the products they sold not just with their names but also with the place and date of manufacture – even the name of the emperor. The practice was labelling as we now know it, and employed visual devices as the kernel of commercial identity. This is the realm of the 'trademark', which has been joined more recently by 'brandmark', a new word that is beginning to do to 'logo' what 'logo' once did to 'symbol'.

The recognition that trademarks had their own value and needed to be protected came relatively recently in the nineteenth century. In a seemingly innocuous event in commercial history, a red triangle locked together with the signature of the word 'Bass' was registered by the eponymous brewery in 1875. In this, the first registration of a trademark, we see the beginnings of an important formal distinction between the use of makers' marks as symbols of product value and as mere conveyors of information. The commercial power of the symbol was dawning.

Business identity styles became more geometric and simplified as art nouveau waned towards the end of the nineteenth century. In 1907, another significant step in the progress of commercial graphic design was taken when Peter Behrens, designer of the trademark symbol for AEG, made it part of a comprehensive design scheme in which he applied the symbol to all print work, products and architecture for the company. This was the first complete corporate identity system.

The distinction between information and persuasion has continued. Symbols that are used to distinguish, label or indicate category are useful in the control and functioning of an ordered society – a bit like filing. This informative role has spawned all sorts of specialist designs, which have had their own line of evolution, particularly in the form of the pictograms and computer icons of the present day. In functional symbols there are no hidden agendas; what you see is what you get. In fact, clarity is everything, and the ambiguities and competitive subtleties of trademark symbols are deliberately missing.

Trademark symbols, on the other hand, trigger emotions through the allusions inherent in their design or by the associations they build up over time as they come to epitomize the spirit and reputation of what they represent. This is part of branding, where brandmarks have become a subset of trademarks and are thus prized as assets in themselves – in some cases, the most valuable asset a company may possess.

Functional symbols

So, functional symbols are those graphic devices that are not invested with any power other than their overt function. They represent or replace words of language in order to concentrate meaning more efficiently so that it can be understood, at a single glance, by anyone from anywhere. Although they are not represented in this book, they nevertheless contribute to, and use, the same assumptions of meaning that effect the design of trademark or brand symbols.

Often the work of the same designers as the creators of trademark symbols, functional symbols are everywhere. Public signs, especially on roads, have a language of symbols that changes and develops as people learn and become more adept at interpreting it. As with any language, the intention is for the symbols to be understood instinctively, without having to think about how. The meaning of an arrow used as a symbol of movement and precise direction on a road sign is obvious, even though the original object has not been commonplace for over three centuries. Visual literacy also allows the arrow to be used for trademark symbols.

A language consisting of graphic symbols that could be understood anywhere on the planet was the dream of many leading designers of the modernist movement in the last century. In the 1970s, American industrial designer Henry Dreyfuss published an exhaustive 'dictionary' of graphic symbols that he had collected and codified by meaning and categorized by use.[2] The belief was that these could be the basis of a universal means of communication, the prelude to a more generalized way of communicating, seen by some as liberating humanity from the straitjacket of specialization. However, this was before the actual practice of globalization superseded the assumptions and boundaries of modernist universality, when the dream began to die along with many of the purist tenets of the movement. Maybe it is just hibernating while the media – the Internet, mobile communications and computing, satellite positioning and navigation – catch up.

The limitations of the symbol language are illustrated by the road sign next to a bus lane or parking bay that consists of a symbol with, underneath it, the words 'at any time' – a kind of *reductio ad absurdum*, especially for anyone who doesn't know what the symbol means in the first place. However, the failure of a system of functional symbols to become a global language has not been due to the failure of individual symbols, which continue to be used and refined as visual literacy develops around the world.

Computer icons, another family of functional symbols, were born towards the end of the last century. The Mac icons invented by Susan Kara for Apple Computers in the early 1980s were part of the revolutionary Macintosh interface. Along with the computer mouse, the appeal of these simple, intuitive symbols helped to turn what was a frighteningly complicated machine into a docile, friendly piece of fruit. With ever increasing sophistication fuelled by the competitive war between the Mac Operating System and

Microsoft's Windows series, the development of computer-screen icons has continued the trend of helping to bring the computer closer and closer to becoming part of our bodies and brains.

Incidentally, the core definition of the word 'icon' has developed in two different directions into two new and seemingly unconnected meanings. The original icon was a sacred representation of a Biblical scene or figure painted on a small wooden panel and venerated in the Orthodox and Catholic Churches. The idea of the icon as a small image signifying a greater power was hubristically appropriated by the designers of computer-screen symbols to convey the potential or power that may be tapped by the click of a mouse. And the meaning of 'icon' as something venerated has come to be used to describe anyone or anything of godlike status in popular culture, from classic cars to star celebs.

Codes and practice

With this proliferation of symbols replacing words in so many aspects of life, graphic designers have claimed semiology – the analysis of signs and symbols, originally confined to literature but increasingly adapted and applied across most cultural forms – for its relevance to their work.

As graphic design becomes one of the most important communication disciplines, applicable to practically every aspect of culture, the temptation is to define visual semiotics in this specific context. This would give the graphic designer an academically approved understanding of what signs mean, in theory providing a formal set of tools and the skills to incorporate them meaningfully into design work.

However, semiotic codes are systems of signs that involve relationships and meaning, and are partly subjective and partly objective. So, comprehending a visual grammar of ideas is difficult because the creation of graphic images depends on conceptual, social, emotional, implied and thematic meanings. Semiotics cannot be easily adapted and applied to graphics until new codes are defined that embrace specifics such as visual structure, typography, photography and colour.

Design and its messages are also relative. The way people receive several meanings from visual messages and interpret them differently is semiotically complex. Nevertheless it is a process that is changing ways of understanding the world, and will eventually, inevitably, require a specific and effective semiotic framework.

Trademark symbols

In a world of persuasion, commercial, political and ideological advocates vie for the attention of the public. It is here that we find those symbols that are designed as bewitching devices to bestow on their owners the far-reaching implications of power. This is a take on the phrase 'potent symbol', which is a tautology; by definition, trademark symbols have power.

Paul Rand, whose work included trademarks for IBM, UPS, Westinghouse and ABC, was one of the great exponents of graphic design in the high modernist period of the latter part of the twentieth century. His designs helped set the styles that endure to this day, characterized by simplicity, neutrality and clarity with an added measure of wit and playfulness. On the power of the trademark, he wrote:

'A trademark is not merely a device to adorn a letterhead, to stamp on a product, or to insert at the base of an advertisement; nor one whose sole prerogative is to imprint itself by dint of constant repetition on the mind of the consumer public. The trademark is a potential illustrative feature of unappreciated vigour and efficacy; and when used as such escapes its customary fate of being a boring restatement of the identity of the product's maker.' [3]

In the competitive world of commerce, it is crucial for a product's maker to be seen as unique, or at least different. And the more distinct that difference, the better. Where the common man is the market, the full potency of the graphic symbol is realized in those marks of identity that are trademarks or brandmarks. The emotional – some say spiritual – power of the symbol creates and consolidates a sense of belonging and so inspires allegiance and loyalty.

The use of the symbol as a tool of business began as a mark of ownership but soon became a mark of trade as well. It has long been connected with the modern idea of branding, and the word 'brand', like symbol itself, has changed its meaning over time. For most of the last century 'brand' meant the image of a product in the market – the kind of psychological disposition it generated in people through its definition and reputation, and its visual representation by a trademark or brandmark.

The origins of branding, literally the marks of ranch ownership seared on the rumps of cows with a branding iron, give us an idea of just how long the symbol has been recognized as a tool of commerce and trade. The emotional point of the brand is: who the cow belonged to might also signify how good the beef was. So the brandmark was not simply a way of recognizing which cows belonged to whom but also, by extension, how valuable they were in the market.

The notion of the brand experience, which is now combined with the idea of brand image in the marketplace, was a sophistication of brand creation and analysis. So the brand has become a symbolic idea or feeling created in the minds of the public, and consists of all the information and expectations associated with a product or service.

With the increasing importance of the brand as a concept, the stock of the graphic symbol as its representative also began to ascend. In the symbol you see how you feel about the brand; it is the epitome of the brand's essence.

Because branding works for products and services, the same initiative, using the same precepts, is applied in other sectors – for example, by corporations and cultural institutions, professional associations, and towns and cities. So 'branding' has become the term for this completeness. And the visual mark that represents it has become the 'brandmark', jostling with 'symbol', 'logo' and 'trademark' in the never-ending search for advantage and marketplace 'cool'.

The art of commercial identity has come full circle, from the significant marks of gods and rulers, to the early visual marks of business and on up to the modern brandmarks that dominate the dreams and lives of today's committed consumers. Nike, the Greek goddess of victory, has transformed into Nike the all-conquering athlete's brand symbolized by the swoosh mark that is recognized the world over, the famous attentions of anti-globalization critics notwithstanding.

Symbol forms

A study of the top 1000 companies in the United States revealed that around a quarter of them had symbol trademarks (11 per cent of these were abstract, such as Chase Manhattan's and 13 per cent representational or pictorial such as Apple's). Another 14 per cent had composites of symbol and name, and the rest had logotypes that used names or initials.

Alan Fletcher, whose work included identity design for Reuters, the Victoria & Albert Museum and ABB, was one of Britain's leading, if most idiosyncratic, graphic designers, who had studied in the United States with luminaries Paul Rand and Josef Albers. He was a knowledgeable judge of what made a symbol work:

'Commercial symbols are like people. Some are reasonably put together but lack personality, others are aggressive, or pompous, or merely unpleasant. Occasionally one encounters an interesting character. Whatever the case, to be effective, a trademark must meet a set of criteria: the utilitarian values of being relevant, appropriate and practical and the intangible qualities of being memorable and distinctive; and that something extra, the visual tweak which creates a unique personality.' [4]

From being an all-embracing term for any visual device of identity, worship or language to becoming a niche definition as a single abstract representation of the spirit of a group, company or alliance, the symbol is graphic design at its most refined. The symbols gathered by Angus Hyland and Steven Bateman in this book are divided into the abstract, based on shapes and geometry, and the representational, based on pictorial forms.

To some the abstract symbol is the purest form of trademark representation. The geometrical forms involved include squares, circles and triangles – the classics of Bauhaus design theory – and variations on these, as well as arrows,

dots, rings and many others. The abstract design allows for interpretation; its meaning is not set – until, that is, it becomes the unique signature of the organization or brand it represents. The circle, for instance, may be used because it symbolizes containment or inner strength, or it may represent the planet, thereby suggesting international or global reach. But these codes are far from clear and most symbols based on the circle are created for arbitrary reasons of taste or whim.

Symbols categorized as abstract forms adopt mostly a hard-edged machine regularity and simplicity, which appeals to a sense of order and certainty while allowing them to be reproduced easily and efficiently. As such, they are also the inheritors of Mies Van Der Rohe's famous modernist tenet: 'Less is more.' Where for over a century the trademark symbol has been reproduced in print, and designed to be so, the abstract symbol meets the present and future by lending itself more readily to the television and computer screen, mainly because it can be animated more freely.

Representational or pictorial forms deliver more literal takes on the name or activity of the owner. Seminal examples are the Apple symbol with a bite out of it, signifying the partaking of the tree of knowledge. The Shell mark is now so well recognized that the company name has been dropped entirely, without any loss of power. This first happened after the introduction of the 1940s version created by Raymond Loewy, probably best known as the designer of Greyhound buses, Studebaker cars, and streamlined trains, including the wonderful Pennsylvania S1.

Alan Fletcher suggested that the rose was the classic example of something commonplace if beautiful that moves easily into the symbolic.[5] A rose is a rose is a flower of course, but it has a distinguished record as an easily referenced symbol. Its five petals were identified with the five wounds of Jesus on the cross. The pinkness of the classic rose gave its colour to the French language – and wine. In England, roses stood for the royal houses of York (white) and Lancaster (red) and thus became competing symbols of allegiance in the Wars of the Roses – still serving the two counties today. A rose is also a delicate English maiden. A red rose is a symbol of love especially favoured on St Valentine's Day, while a white rose is a symbol of chastity. And as an emblem, the rose is deployed for the England rugby team and as a trademark for Cadbury Roses chocolates.

Twenty-first-century moves

Once just stamped or painted, then printed, symbols now have to be designed for an unprecedented diversity of media. The requirement is for them to read well at extreme sizes, formats and resolutions – as a menu icon on a mobile phone, on the URL bar of a website, as a TV or movie ident as well as in print.

The impact of digital media is not confined solely to how a symbol can be made to behave within its various applications. The computer also has a profound and productive impact on the working practices of graphic designers. Profound because those most laborious effects and illusions that previously could not be attempted without help can be achieved quickly and precisely; productive because ideas can be transformed into reality and then applied efficiently in the flash of a keyboard stroke and mouse click.

The demand for symbols to be effective in a greater range of media and sizes requires that symbol design continues to evolve. Where once the designer might have exploited the increasing availability of colour in the printing process, now there is the opportunity to digitally engineer a symbol to work on the dynamic interfaces of mobile phones, Internet sites and 3-D virtual environments. Designing for multilayered (build-up) or time-based (animated) effects has moved from a fringe requirement to the mainstream in the first decade of the twenty-first century.

Cultures change and styles change – often so gradually that hardly anyone notices. But, as ever, the avant-garde eventually becomes the convention. Yet many of the quirkier, most distinctive symbols of the twentieth century would not get a look-in today at the reviewing committees of commissioning companies or their marketing departments. Perhaps the facility that digital processing technology grants to the twenty-first-century designer has enriched the cleverness of, yet impoverished, the range of symbols. Is a symbol now animated to catch the eye, or just to compensate for its unremarkable design?

To work for its living, a symbol has to be seen; in fact, it must be highly exposed. Repetition and recognition are what it is designed for, so that it can build a bond with the emotional dispositions of the consumer's mind. Without that, its meaning, its interpretation, the artfulness of its form and its cleverness are nothing. How much of the power of the symbol is understood by the public, or even the designer, is moot. Often the creators of graphic symbols, working to a client's brief, will admire only the neatness of form and the encapsulation of an idea, rather than the power it will bestow in determining the fortunes of the client.

Delving into these questions of power, overt and covert, that symbols represent, designer Lora Starling describes, and warns of, deeper influences inherent in the symbol than are generally supposed. Here, we move from the idea that the power of visual identity lies somewhere in the same emotional realm as seeing an old friend in a familiar suit to the post-religious, post-rationalist mystical idea that a trademark symbol has an aura of indefinable but determining energy.[6] Who knows? But just as the acceptance of the conceptual and abstract as legitimate in art is accelerating, so we may soon know which way the wind is blowing.

It is certainly true that as modernism loses its grip on the imagination and education of designers, more intuitive and less prescriptive parameters are being used to judge the efficacy of symbol forms. If semiotic theory is created specifically for, rather than adapted to, graphic design,

then a usable set of tools for comprehending the symbolism of symbols can be built up and disseminated to create a standard, and thus universally understood, visual language.

For each generation, the call of originality and newness is defining. People who think they know differently from what went before often get to be designers. After all, designers want to be responsible for making something entirely fresh out of nothing. Despite warnings that 'nothing is new', creating a symbol goes a long way towards scratching that itch.

A transformation of the symbol, from a general mark into a specific graphic form, has taken place. The simplicity of the symbol lends itself to ubiquity with its propagation through print, mass production, television and the computer screen. Much is invested in its creation because it wields power – and thus makes money. As a visible device that represents an abstract idea, the symbol does not just derive power by expressing the qualities of its owner, it also creates its own.

1   Eric Gill, *An Essay on Typography*, Sheed & Ward, London, 1931.
2   Henry Dreyfuss, *Symbol Sourcebook*, McGraw-Hill Book Company, New York, 1972.
3   Egbert Jacobson (ed.), *Seven Designers Look at Trademark Design*, Paul Theobald, Chicago, 1952.
4   David Gibbs (ed. for Pentagram), *The Compendium*, Phaidon Press, London, 1993.
5   Germano Facetti and Alan Fletcher, *Identity Kits: A Pictorial Survey of Visual Signs*, Studio Vista, 1971.
6   Lora Starling, *The Logo Decoded*, Alchemist Four, 2008.

David Gibbs is a senior writer, editor and communications strategist who has worked with many of the leading designers in Britain and America. Collaborating with David Hillman, he wrote the best-selling *Century Makers* on 100 things that changed our lives in the twentieth century. Other books include *Nova*, a look back at the iconoclastic magazine of the 1960s, and *The Compendium*, a major survey of the work of Pentagram.

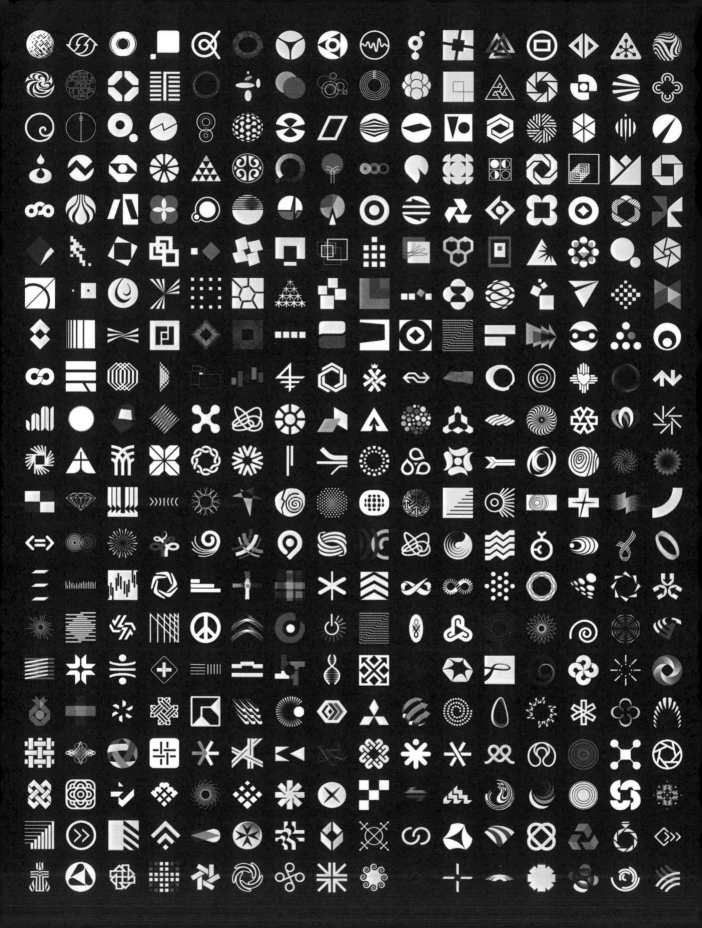

ABSTRACT

1.

2.

3.

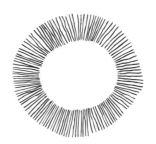

4.

5.

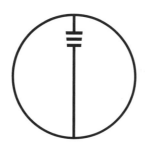

6.

7.

8.

9.

10.

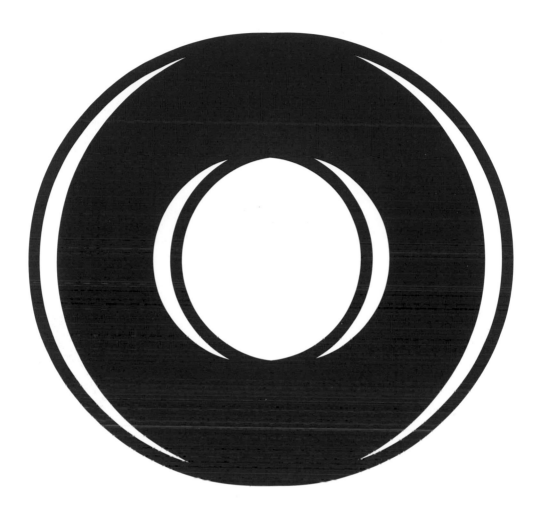

1. **MicroPlace** finance, USA
   Attik, UK/USA, 2007
   A warm, optimistic symbol for an organization
   whose aim is to alleviate global poverty by
   enabling everyday people to invest in the world's
   working poor.

2. **KartaMira Travel Company** tourism, Ukraine
   Headshot brand development, Ukraine, 2008
   A series of overlapping circles suggests myriad
   journeys around the world.

3. **Replenish UK** health and beauty, UK
   Naughtyfish design, Australia, 2001
   An illustrated circular motif supports the natural
   ingredients promoted by this beauty product
   brand.

4. **Luses** music, Finland
   Hahmo, Finland, 2005
   A circular musical stave represents the
   Foundation for the Promotion of Finnish Music.

5. **Süddeutscher Rundfunk** broadcasting, Germany
   Stankowski + Duschek, Germany, 1954
   A simple image of an antenna for a radio and
   television broadcaster.

6. **Septemvri** manufacturing, Bulgaria
   Stefan Kanchev, Bulgaria, c.1960s–1970s
   Symbol for a manufacturer of steel pipes.

7. **East Coast Radio** broadcasting, South Africa
   Mister Walker, South Africa, 2005
   Symbol suggesting the radiating signal (and
   perhaps rising sun); designed for Durban's
   number one radio station.

8. **Target** retail, USA
   Unimark International, USA, 1970
   To maintain consistency across the Target brand,
   Unimark/Chicago simplified the symbol for this
   historic American supermarket chain; it is still in
   use today.

9. **Journal of the History of Biology** publishing, USA
   David Ford, USA, 1968
   Published by Springer, this internationally
   acclaimed scientific journal has used the same
   mark for over four decades.

10. **Macquarie Bank** finance, Australia
    Cato Partners, Australia, 1984
    Named after Australia's currency founder,
    this symbol recalls the country's first currency:
    the 'holey dollar'.

11.

12.

13.

14.

15.

16.

17.

18.

11. Thomas Kolb consultancy, Germany
*Büro Uebele Visuelle Kommunikation,
Germany, 2004*
Symbol for a 'building biologist' who provides
advice on how to create a healthy home.
The mark finds inspiration in the archetypal natural
house: a snail shell.

12. Cycle Sports Schöftland retail, Switzerland
Neeser & Müller, Switzerland, 1996
A link from a bicycle chain clearly identifies
the business of this bicycle shop in northern
Switzerland.

13. Evotec AG medical research, Germany
KMS TEAM, Germany, 1999
The circles symbolize potential, hinting at the
new drugs and therapies developed as a result
of Evotec's work.

14. Fondazione Querini Stampalia arts and
culture, Italy
Studio Camuffo, Italy, 2001
A distinctly modern mark for an archive, library,
and museum in an historic Venetian house;
it reflects renovation work and embellishments
introduced by the 20th-century Italian architect
Carlo Scarpa.

15. La Fondation Motrice charity, France
Landor Associates, international, 2007
Symbol for a French charity aiming to improve
the quality of life for those suffering from
cerebral palsy.

16. GMDRDP public services, UK
Funnel Creative, UK, 2007
Uniting the various drug action teams of Greater
Manchester, this symbol reflects the initiative's
full-service approach to drug treatment and
reducing deaths.

17. Gaia Access Project events, Japan
Ken Miki & Associates, Japan, 1993
Symbol for an event promoting environmental
issues.

18. Metlink transport, Australia
Cornwell Design, Australia, 2005
This symbol is part of a comprehensive identity
programme for 'the Met' aimed at reflecting a
much improved service.

19.

20.

21.

22.

19. Better Place energy, USA
Addis Creson, USA, 2008
Symbol for a clean energy brand representing
a desired global move from petrol pump to
electricity plug.

20. Boston retail, Poland
Karol Sliwka, Poland, 1992
A simple, dynamic mark for a high street retailer
of audio-visual equipment.

21. La Gaceta de los Negocios newspapers, Spain
Cruz más Cruz, Spain, 1992
A simple profit-chart motif proved the perfect
solution for Spain's leading daily financial
newspaper.

22. Statistics Norway government, Norway
Enzo Finger Design, Norway, 1993
A minimal symbol clearly communicates the
client's mission to deliver accurate, dependable
statistics.

23. Fantini Elettronica healthcare, Italy
Brunazzi&Associati, Italy, 1964
An electronic pulse symbolizes the products
manufactured by this Milanese company.

24. Under Graph music, Japan
Good Design Company, Japan, 2004
A literal interpretation of a Japanese rock
band's name.

25. Cukiernia Jotka food and beverages, Poland
Karol Sliwka, Poland, 1984
A bold, abstract symbol for a confectioner
and patisserie.

26. Avit publishing, Poland
Karol Sliwka, Poland, 1990
A striking symbol for a Polish publishing house.

27. Kavir Tire Company manufacturing, Iran
Ebrahim Haghighi, Iran, 1985
Bold geometric forms are cleverly combined to
suggest a moving wheel.

28. Victorian Cytology Service healthcare, Australia
Sadgrove Design, Australia, 1991
Symbol for Australia's largest cytology test
laboratory.

23.

24.

25.

26.

27.

28.

Transport for London

Public transport, UK
Edward Johnston, UK, 1916–19

The world-famous 'roundel' device has its origins in platform signs designed in the early twentieth century to identify stations on the London Underground rail network. The bar and circle, as it was then known, comprised a solid red enamel disc and a blue horizontal bar upon which the station name appeared.

Designed to distinguish the station name from the myriad type styles and imagery of surrounding advertisements, the bar and circle provided the inspiration for today's roundel, designed by Edward Johnston (1872–1944) between 1916 and 1919. Having been commissioned to design a new typeface by the Underground's publicity manager, Frank Pick (1878–1941), Johnston also updated the bar and circle motif, which he referred to as a 'bulls-eye'. By 1917 he had reworked its proportions to accommodate the new typeface and Underground logotype; the red disc became a circle and the new symbol was registered as a trademark.

Officially signed off in 1919, the new roundel was applied across publicity material and began to appear on station exteriors and platforms from the early 1920s. Today, it is used across the entire Transport for London (TfL) network, with changes in colour distinguishing particular modes of transport. For example, the Underground still has a blue bar and a red circle, Tramlink has a bright green circle and a blue bar, London buses have an all-red symbol and the core TfL symbol is all blue.

BUSES

COACHES

CYCLE HIRE

DIAL·A·RIDE

DLR

OVERGROUND

PRIVATE HIRE

TRAMLINK

STREETS

TAXIS

RIVER

UNDERGROUND

®

London Transport, poster by Man Ray, 1938.

29.

30.

31.

32.

33.

34.

35.

36.

37.

38.

39.

29. **Coloplast** healthcare, Denmark
Hans Due, Denmark, 1988
A 'global' mark suggests the international reach of a brand specializing in colostomy and other healthcare products.

30. **Rock Institute** education, USA
John Rieben/University of Wisconsin–Madison Department of Art, USA, 1995
Symbol for an educational facility focusing on 'earth science' studies.

31. **Red Eléctrica de España** energy, Spain
Cruz más Cruz, Spain, 1987
Dynamic symbol for the corporation responsible for Spain's power transmission system and electricity grid.

32. **CEZA** property, Poland
Karol Sliwka, Poland, 1991
Evocative symbol for a company renting office premises and warehouses.

33. **Powiatowa Spóldzielnia Pracy Uslug Odziezowo-Skórzanych** manufacturing, Poland
Karol Sliwka, Poland, 1964
Symbol representing a manufacturer of leather clothing and accessories.

34. **Louisiana Land and Exploration** energy/exploration, USA
Arnold Saks Associates, USA, 1976
Fluid shapes suggest the natural resources desired by this oil and gas exploration company.

35. **Science and Art** publishing, Bulgaria
Stefan Kanchev, Bulgaria, c.1960s–70s
A dynamic mark suggesting progress and creativity.

36. **Macel Pin** energy, Croatia
Likovni Studio, Croatia, 2003
A simple, stylized illustration of a flame for a company distributing gas equipment.

37. **Norsk Films AS** film, Norway
Paul Brand, Norway, 1968
A camera lens and its aperture provide the inspiration for this symbol.

38. **L'Hotel du Lac** hospitality, Japan
Ken Miki & Associates, Japan, 2004
A stylized flower expresses a modern, aspirational tone for a luxury hotel.

39. **Multicultural Arts Victoria**
arts and culture, Australia
Cato Partners, Australia, 2009
A graphic representation of global cultures being attracted to and converging on the state of Victoria.

40.

41.

40. Epiderm healthcare, Australia
Cato Partners, Australia, 2006
An organization awarding grants to scientific research, education programmes and public relations activities.

41. For Company Management finance, Poland
Logotypy.com, Poland, 2007
A complex symbol expresses the innovative, forward-thinking approach of this financial consultancy.

42. Bank Direct finance, New Zealand
Cato Partners, Australia, 1997
The symbol for New Zealand's first 'virtual' bank combines technology with a globe.

43. 21st Century Museum of Contemporary Art, Kanazawa arts and culture, Japan
Taku Satoh Design Office Inc., Japan, 2004
Framed artworks reflect the work on display at this gallery of international contemporary art.

44. Jernova food and beverages, Ukraine
Artemov Artel, Ukraine, 2007
A rustic mark reflects the use of traditional millstones and certified organic corn, and bread baked in firewood ovens.

45. Zee retail, Switzerland
Vingtneuf degres sàrl, Switzerland, 2008
A playful, creative symbol supports the designer toy brand's 'art is medicine' strapline. Commissioned by Characterstation.com.

46. Retallack Hotel & Spa hospitality, UK
Absolute Design, UK, 2007
A modern symbol for a luxury resort in Cornwall recalls the county's proud Celtic heritage.

47. TVL licensing, UK
The Partners, UK, 2008
New symbol for the UK's TV licensing body based on the universal icon for a power button; the tick conveys a sense of positive responsibility.

42.

43.

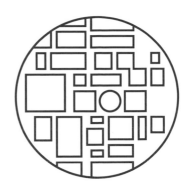

44.

45.

46.

47.

48.

49.

50.

51.

48. Souperie restaurants, Estonia
LOOVVOOL, Estonia, 2007
Customers combine different soups at this
gourmet takeaway. A series of circles symbolizes
the choices.

49. AFF consultancy, Norway
Mission Design, Norway, 2004
Water ripples this management consultancy's
focus on self-development through shared
insights and experiences.

50. Tram SA transport, Greece
HGV Pierre Vermeir, UK, 2004
The symbol for a public tram system in Athens
suggests the journey and tracks.

51. Moshi Moshi Mind fashion/healthcare, Denmark
Designbolaget, Denmark, 2008
Simple geometric forms mirror the holistic
approach of a fashion and well-being brand.

52. Global Waste Technologies recycling, UK
Ranch, UK, 2008
Three overlapping circles suggest themes
of renewal and continuity; the bold execution
further supports the company's innovative spirit.

53. Peapod transport, USA
Arnell, USA, 2009
A playful mark symbolizing an innovative
'neighbourhood electric vehicle'.

54. LifeSensor technology, Germany
KMS TEAM, Germany, 2007
Symbol for a web-based application allowing
users to compile personal health histories.
The intersecting circles form a 'medical' cross
while alluding to information transfer and privacy
control. Commissioned by Inter Component
Ware AG.

55. Lapponia House property development, Finland
Porkka & Kuutsa, Finland, 1999
Cloudberries are a Lapland delicacy and provide
the inspiration for a symbol supporting the client's
desire to enhance its customer's 'joy for life'
through sustainable architecture.

52.

53.

54.

55.

CND (Campaign for Nuclear Disarmament)

Non-profit organization, UK
Gerald Holtom, UK, 1958

Organized by the Direct Action Committee Against Nuclear War, the first Aldermaston march took place on Easter weekend, 4–7 April 1958. Several thousand people took part in the inaugural 52-mile march from Trafalgar Square to the Atomic Weapons Research Establishment at Aldermaston in Berkshire. The first four-day march captured the public's imagination and, at their height during the early 1960s, subsequent marches attracted tens of thousands of activists. A familiar sight at those marches – and at any peace march since – was the nuclear disarmament symbol designed by Gerald Holtom (1914–85).

A professional artist and designer, Holtom was a graduate of the RCA and, as a conscientious objector to war, an ideal candidate to design a symbol for the Aldermaston march. Combining the semaphore letters 'N' (the angled, downward strokes) and 'D' (the vertical stroke) to spell 'Nuclear Disarmament', Holtom designed one of history's most recognizable symbols. Holtom explained that the design was intended to symbolize a 'human being in despair' with outstretched arms. However, he later expressed regret at the element of despair in a letter to his friend, the American pacifist Ken Kolsbun, saying he would have liked to have inverted the symbol to suggest a more positive, proactive tone.

Although initially designed at the behest of the Direct Action Committee, the symbol wasn't copyrighted and was adopted by the Campaign For Nuclear Disarmament, also founded in 1958. Still used by the CND, Holtom's symbol has transcended its intended use and is now recognized across the globe as a symbol for peace in general, as well as for the ongoing campaign for nuclear disarmament.

1.

2.

3.

4.

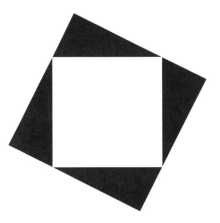

5.

6.

7.

1. **Rochester Institute of Technology**
    education, USA
    R. Roger Remington, USA, 1969
    A distinctly modern mark conveys the innovative
    spirit championed by RIT. The symbol's designer
    is currently Professor of Graphic Design at RIT.
2. **Museo Fotografia Contemporanea**
    arts and culture, Italy
    Studio FM Milano, Italy, 2004
    Negative space suggests the outline of an artwork
    for a gallery showcasing contemporary photography.

3. **Commonwealth Bank** finance, Australia
    Cato Partners, Australia, 1997
    Symbol based on the five stars of the Southern
    Cross constellation; it communicates an historical
    statement in a contemporary manner.
4. **Ontera** manufacturing, Australia
    THERE, Australia, 2009
    Two squares refer to the products created by the
    largest manufacturer of modular carpet tiles in
    Australia and New Zealand.

5. **Hans Kjell Larsen** architecture, Norway
    Paul Brand, Norway, 1970
    Bold mark designed for an Oslo architecture firm.
6. **Prefna n.p.** construction, Slovakia
    Frantisek Boban, Slovakia, 1965
    Symbol for a company specializing in building
    products.
7. **Orma (Brescia)** manufacturing, Italy
    A.G. Fronzoni, Italy, 1957
    Symbol for a manufacturer of pressed and
    rolled metals.

Deutsche Bank

Finance, Germany
Anton Stankowski, Germany, 1974

Anton Stankowski was a founding partner of German design firm Stankowski + Duschek and one of the true giants of corporate identity design; that *Symbol* is peppered with examples of their work is testament to their expertise in this area. However, the symbol highlighted here is arguably one of the finest corporate marks ever designed.

Deutsche Bank is one of the world's leading providers of financial solutions, a European global powerhouse serving the financial needs of corporations, firms, institutions and private and business clients worldwide. When the bank was founded in 1870 an Imperial eagle led its identity; this was succeeded in 1918 by an oval containing the initials 'DB'. Although there was a brief return to the eagle, the 'DB' initials on an oval ground remained the bank's core identity for many years. By the 1970s the banking industry was changing and Deutsche Bank identified the need for a new symbol – one that reflected the changing times, an extended service palette, the introduction of modern techniques and technologies and increasing globalization.

Eight designers were invited to submit designs and when Stankowski's was selected it reflected the bank's positive attitude towards progress and change – it is bold and simple, yet it must have taken many by surprise. The diagonal stands for consistent growth and dynamic development, while the square suggests security; on its website, Deutsche Bank summarizes the symbol as representing 'dynamic growth in a stable environment'. It sought an identity that was easy to apply in any medium, striking, unmistakable, free of any 'fashionable' accent and able to stand the test of time. Stankowski met the brief perfectly and the resulting symbol speaks for itself in any language. In 2010 Deutsche Bank relaunched its brand and visual identity so that the symbol – unchanged since 1974 – is used independently of the Deutsche Bank logotype, in line with other global superbrands and reflecting Stankowski's original recommendation.

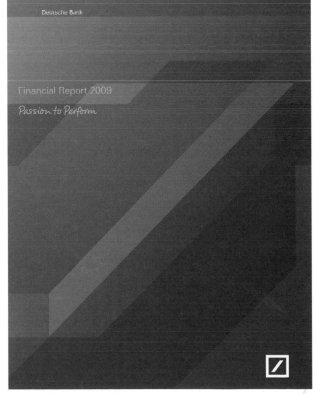

1974

2010

8.

9.

8. **Registro Tumori del Piemonte e Valle d'Aosta** healthcare, Italy
Brunazzi&Associati, Italy, 1971
Mark for a cancer register and research institute in Turin. The geometrical progression represents developments in research and documentation.

9. **Narodna Prosveta** publishing, Bulgaria.
Stefan Kanchev, Bulgaria, c.1960s–70s
Dynamic mark for a Bulgarian publisher.

10. **Permanent Concrete** construction, Canada
Chris Yaneff Ltd, Canada, 1970
A solid, architectural mark for an Ontario company producing ready-mixed concrete.

11. **RKW** professional associations, Germany
Stankowski + Duschek, Germany, 1968–90
Association supporting small and medium-sized businesses.

12. **Pongauer Holzbau** construction, Austria
Modelhart Design, Austria, 2005
Mark symbolizing a building and a timber profile, designed for a company employing traditional techniques to design and build wooden houses.

13. **First Bank** finance, USA
Arnold Saks Associates, USA, 1966
A strong square built around a smaller square conveys a sense of security.

14. **Market Squared** consultancy, UK
Applied Works, UK, 2005
Drawing on the typical road layout of a Roman market town (roads laid noth–south and east–west with the market square in the centre), this symbol was designed for a consultancy providing advice on how to create successful markets in the UK and continental Europe.

15. **Landesausstellung Niedersachsen** arts and culture, Germany
Stankowski + Duschek, Germany, 1985
Symbol for a state show (county fair) in Germany's Lower Saxony region.

16. **Mikkeli City** tourism, Finland
Kari Piippo, Finland, 2001
Symbol inspired by the city's grid plan and coat of arms (from which the bow motif derives). It is usually seen in blue, which represents the city's lakes and the Finnish flag.

17. **Student library** education/libraries, Bulgaria
Stefan Kanchev, Bulgaria, c.1960s–70s
A dynamic symbol suggesting rows of bookshelves.

18. **Grebennikov** publishing, Russia and Germany
Ony, Russia, 2007
A stylized open book with a bookmark is the symbol for a publisher of books on management, marketing and human resources.

19. **Silistra (Lipa)** manufacturing, Bulgaria
Stefan Kanchev, Bulgaria, c.1960s–70s
A solid symbol for a furniture factory: *Lipa* is Slavic for the *Tilia* (also called lime or linden) tree, which in Slavic mythology was considered sacred.

20. **Kihara Project Office Inc.** town planning, Japan
Ken Miki & Associates, Japan, 1991
A simple arrangement of squares for an architectural planning group.

21. **Akademie für Bildende Künste Johannes Gutenberg Universität Mainz**
education, Germany
Stankowski + Duschek, Germany, 2001
Minimal mark for an applied arts school in the historic Rhineland town of Mainz.

10.

11.

12.

13.

14.

15.

16.

17.

18.

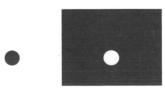

19.

20.

21.

22.

23.

24.

25.

26.

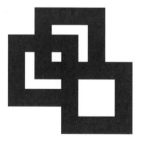

27.

22. Lucy Lee Recordings music, Belgium
Coast, Belgium, 2004
A bold mark for a Brussels-based label
specializing in contemporary club music.

23. Deutsche Rentenversicherung
finance, Germany
KMS TEAM, Germany, 2005
Two fields complement each other, forming a
square and expressing the integrity of this
German pension fund.

24. Thinkbox marketing, UK
KentLyons, UK, 2006
A thought bubble communicates the creative-
thinking theme and client name with clarity.

25. Premier Lifts engineering, UK
A2 Design, UK, 2003
A simple but effective image symbolizing the up/
down nature of this lift business.

26. Third Millennium Gate
property development, Japan
Ken Miki & Associates, Japan, 2000
Symbol for an innovative architectural project
in Osaka.

27. Axalink telecoms, Russia
RockBee Design, Russia, 2008
Four geometric forms arranged at angles suggest
the multiple services provided by this Russian
telecoms brand.

28. Current TV broadcasting, USA
Peter Saville & Brett Wickens, USA/UK, 2005
Symbol suggesting that this groundbreaking
cable network and multimedia brand powered
by user-generated content is awaiting input.

29. Uhlmann Pac-Systeme
manufacturing, Germany
Stankowski + Duschek, Germany, 1986
Still in use, this symbol evokes the products and
associated services provided by a manufacturer
of pharmaceutical packaging machines.

28.

29.

30.

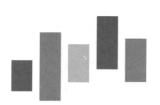

31.

32.

33.

34.

35.

36.

37.

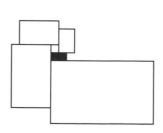

38.

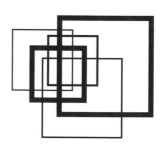

39.

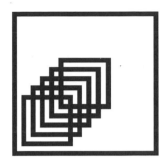

40.

41.

42.

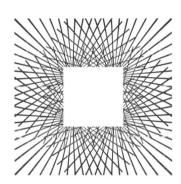

30. Urban Space Commercial Properties
property, USA
Lodge Design, USA, 2004
A playful landscape for a property company
specializing in restaurants, retail and
entertainment spaces.

31. Landkreis Esslingen tourism, Germany
Stankowski + Duschek, Germany, 1990
Contemporary mark hinting at the medieval
heritage of a German town and its
surrounding district.

32. Messe Frankfurt events, Germany
Stankowski + Duschek, Germany, 1983
Colourful boxes suggest the logistics involved in
the work of the world's largest trade-fair organizer
(with its own exhibition grounds in Frankfurt).
The symbol is still in use.

33. Realservice property, Germany
Toman Graphic Design, Czech Republic, 2004
Building blocks avoid the usual estate agent
clichés while clearly communicating the nature
of the business.

34. Inteco telecoms, Germany
Stankowski + Duschek, Germany, 1992
A simple mark made up of small pixel-like squares
for a telecoms and computer-science-systems
company.

35. Mitae information technology, Spain
Zorraquino, Spain, 2005
A pixellated mark supports the client's
technology-led approach.

**36. DAAO (Dictionary of Australian Artists
Online)** arts and culture, Australia
Naughtyfish design, Australia, 2005
A pixelated symbol for an online searchable
archive of Australian art and artists.

37. Marcus Beale Architects Ltd architecture, UK
Applied Works, UK, 2004
A spiral of suitably architectural rectangles whose
proportions derive from the Fibonacci sequence.

38. Ministry of Culture Republic of Croatia
government, Croatia
Designsystem, Croatia, 2001
Symbol suggesting the rich and varied landscape
of 21st-century Croatian culture.

39. Akitt, Swanson + Pearce architecture, Canada
Ernst Barenscher, Canada, 1971
Suggesting architecture and innovation,
the symbol for this Toronto practice is still in
use today.

40. Soft Partner AS information technology,
Denmark
Punktum Design, Denmark, 2002
A dynamic mark suggesting innovation for a
company providing services and administrative IT
systems for small and medium-sized enterprises.

41. Evanston Art Center arts and culture, USA
Jack Weiss Associates, USA, 1986
A vibrant mark representing one of the oldest
and largest visual art centres in Illinois.

42. The Bank of New York finance, USA
Lippincott, USA, 2005
A lively symbol superseded in 2007 after the client
merged with Mellon Bank to become the Bank of
New York Mellon.

MOT

Government/vehicle testing, UK
Jock Kinneir, UK, c.1960

Currently administered by VOSA (Vehicle & Operator Services Agency), the MOT test is an annual examination of automobile safety, roadworthiness and exhaust emissions applicable to most vehicles in the UK over three years old. Wander around the more industrial areas of any UK town or city and you'll see this familiar symbol on the signage of garages both large and small, indicating that they offer MOT testing services. The symbol is an endorsement of roadworthiness, also often displayed on car windscreens.

Look closely at the triangular composition and you might spot the letters 'MOT', indicating the Ministry of Transport, the government department that introduced the test. However, the ubiquitous nature of this symbol and the abstract qualities that make it such a clear and distinctive marque transcend lettering in much the same way, for example, as the International Paper Company symbol designed by Lester Beall in 1960.

Jock Kinneir (1917–94) designed the MOT symbol around the same time, probably during the late 1950s when he was working on a number of projects for the Ministry of Transport and Civil Aviation, a period during which he and Margaret Calvert designed the Transport typeface. MOT tests were introduced in 1960, with Kinneir's symbol the first and only symbol used to identify test centres. Half a century later it is still going strong.

1.

2.

3.

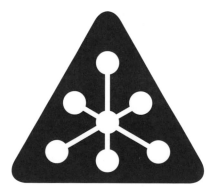

4.

5.

6.

7.

8.

1. **Kaneda Ski Manufacturing Co.**
    sport and leisure, Japan
    Nippon Design Center, Japan, 1969
    A simplified mountain for a manufacturer of skis
    and ski accessories.
2. **Pyramis** finance, USA
    Sullivan, USA, 2006
    A triangle suggests the outline of a pyramid,
    while the shining sun motif sets a distinctly
    positive tone.
3. **ids** media, UK
    Blast, UK, 2008
    ids is a Virgin Media company that sells
    advertising for the Virgin Media group.

4. **MyState** finance, Australia
    Cornwell Design, Australia, 2007
    A new identity following the merger of Tasmania's
    largest credit unions: Islandstate and Connect
    Financial.
5. **Klinikum der Universität Göttingen**
    healthcare, Germany
    Stankowski + Duschek, Germany, 1977
    A distinctive take on a 'medical cross' for a
    university clinical centre.
6. **Civil Airports, Sofia** transport, Bulgaria
    Stefan Kanchev, Bulgaria, c.1960s–70s
    An elegant symbol evoking the romance of flight.

7. **Hager Tehalit** technology, Germany
    Stankowski + Duschek, Germany, 1998
    Dynamic mark for a leading supplier of solutions
    and services for residential, commercial and
    industrial electrotechnical installations.
8. **SEL** communications, Germany
    Stankowski + Duschek, Germany, 1954–81
    A striking mark inspired by emanating signals.

9.

10.

11.

12.

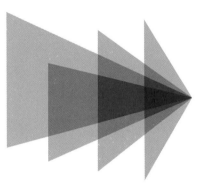

13.

14.

15.

9. **CSB** finance, USA
Unimark International, USA, c.1970s
A striking and distinctly positive mark designed
for the Colorado State Bank.

10. **SCA** paper, Sweden
Pentagram, UK, 1990
Symbol representing the paper group's three
spearhead businesses: graphic paper, packaging
and hygiene.

11. **ArtsBoston** arts and culture, USA
Alphabet Arm, USA, 2009
Leading online resource for arts and
entertainment listings in Boston.

12. **BPRI** consultancy, UK
The Partners, UK, 2006
Four triangles converge on a single point,
symbolizing the pinpointed clarity offered by this
research-led consultancy.

13. **Young Presidents Association** professional
associations, USA
Danne Design, USA, 1985
This organization of young business leaders
conducts educational initiatives aimed at training
better executives for the future.

14. **Kumba Resources** mining, South Africa
Mister Walker, South Africa, 2001
One of the triangle's dots is in a different colour
to indicate precious ore hidden beneath the
earth's surface.

15. **Mori no 10-kyo** property development, Japan
Ken Miki & Associates, Japan, 2007
The symbol designed for this multifamily housing
developer suggests both a house and a family.

Paul Forrer AG

Manufacturing, Switzerland
Ernst Hiestand + Partners, Switzerland, 1996

For a corporate symbol designed in the mid-1990s the mark for Paul Forrer AG – a leading Swiss provider of hydraulic and driveline systems – evokes an aesthetic more in tune with the golden era of corporate identity design: the 1950s to the 1970s. In the late 1990s, prompted by new technologies, more sophisticated software and the advent of the Internet, corporate design and branding generally embraced a more rounded, often three-dimensional, drop-shadowed aesthetic. Some of these identities worked, of course, but many proved every bit as ephemeral as they were on the day they were launched.

Fortunately, designers don't always drink at the same watering hole and whilst embracing these same emerging technologies, some steered well clear of digital-age clichés. The symbol designed in 1996 for Paul Forrer AG is one such example, and reflects the brand's reputation, the simplicity and clarity of its design suggesting notions of efficiency and precision.

With clients in the agricultural, forestry, communal and building sectors, Paul Forrer AG produces professional outdoor motor equipment and tools such as chainsaws, brush-cutters, shredders and snow blowers. However, its main trade is the manufacturing of hydraulics and driveline systems (a driveline comprising the components of a vehicle's drivetrain, excluding the engine and transmission). The symbol represents the dynamic nature and mobile applications of these products, and the truncated arrows suggest the components that enable machines to move forwards and backwards.

1.

2.

3.

4.

5.

6.

1. **Alfa** chemicals, Poland
   Karol Sliwka, Poland, 1990
   A simple kite mark for a company producing household chemicals.
2. **Kurusawa Photo Office** photography, Japan
   Good Design Company, Japan, 2003
   A graphic interpretation of a camera's aperture for this photography studio.

3. **MLC Centre** retail, Australia
   THERE, Australia, 2008
   This symbol reflects the octagonal profile of the skyscraper at the heart of a landmark commercial and retail development in Sydney.
4. **Jyske Bank** finance, Denmark
   Jyske Bank (in-house), Denmark, 1967
   A seemingly timeless design conveys security and continuity for Denmark's second largest independent bank.

5. **Vantage Homebuilders** construction, USA
   John Rieben/Rieben & Craig, USA, 1980
   A bold hexagonal motif suggests both the volume and roofs of the residential properties built by this firm.
6. **The Weather Channel** broadcasting, Australia
   Mark Gowing, Australia, 2003
   A strong mark supports the credentials of Australia's national weather TV network.

7.

8.

9.

10.

11.

12.

7. **Open Source Festival** arts and culture, Germany
Bionic Systems, Germany, 2006
A wound ring with different textures suggests
the coming together of people at this Düsseldorf
music festival.

8. **Centralny Zarzad Spoldzielczos'ci Pracy**
trade, Poland
Stefan Sledzinski, Poland, 1965
Interlocked hexagons express the relationships
fostered by an organization promoting foreign
trade in crafts.

9. **Pheroshop** health and beauty, The Netherlands
unieq, The Netherlands, 2009
The symbol for this expert in strong natural
fragrances recalls the shape of pheromone
receptor cells.

10. **Mas S.A.** health and beauty, Spain
Perez Sanchez, Spain, 1969
Simple geometric mark for a brand of cosmetics
and perfumes.

11. **Northern Corporation of Chemical Industry**
chemicals Bulgaria
Stefan Kanchev, Bulgaria, c.1960s–70s
Linked hexagons suggest a suitably
scientific tone.

12. **Bulgarian Industrial Chamber**
government, Bulgaria
Stefan Kanchev, Bulgaria, c.1960s–70s
A strong geometric mark suggesting
industrial themes.

1.

2.

1. **Santa Fe By Design** manufacturing, USA
   BBDK, Inc. , USA, 2005
   A simple mark for a New Mexico bath-fixtures
   brand suggests water dripping from a tap.

2. **Learning and Performance Consulting Inc.**
   arts and culture/consultancies, Japan
   Taste Inc., Japan, 2005
   A series of ovals conveys a sense of energy
   and creativity.

1.

2.

3.

4.

5.

6.

1. **Canal Metro** broadcasting, Spain
   ruiz+company, Spain, 2000
   A TV screen on a tube; this symbol for a channel
   broadcasting on Barcelona's Underground
   network was commissioned by Transports
   Metropolitan de Barcelona.

2. **Design Centre** arts and culture, Italy
   Unimark International, Italy, c.1970s
   Geometric forms combine to resemble an eye;
   a modern spirit supports the 'design' theme.

3. **Cinepaq** film, Spain
   Cruz más Cruz, Spain, 1989
   Symbol referencing the visual appearance of a film
   reel for a film distribution company.

4. **Lincoln Center for the Performing Arts**
   arts and culture, USA
   Chermayeff & Geismar, USA, 1983
   **Bold symbol reflecting the architecture of one of
   New York's landmark arts centres; the mark has
   since been superseded.**

5. **Expo Optica** events, Spain
   Cruz más Cruz, Spain, 1991
   Three geometric forms combine to create the
   image of an eye for an international optometry fair.

6. **The Chase Manhattan Bank** finance, USA
   Chermayeff & Geismar, USA, 1960
   Iconic symbol introduced following the merger
   of Chase National Bank and the Bank of the
   Manhattan Company. At the time, few American
   corporations used abstract corporate symbols,
   but Tom Geismar's classic design has survived
   the test of time and several mergers to become
   one of the world's most recognizable trademarks.

7.

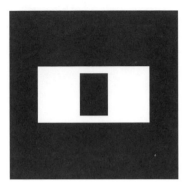

8.

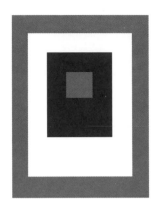

9.

10.

7. **Eyestorm** arts and culture, UK
    Studio Tonne, UK, 2007
    Strong geometric shapes form a pixellated eye
    for the leading online retailer of limited-edition
    contemporary art.
8. **Jan E. Olesen eftft. AS** construction, Denmark
    Punktum Design, Denmark, 2001
    Geometric forms hint at the product of a glazing
    company specializing in bespoke windows
    and doors.

9. **Landesgartenschau Ingolstadt** arts and
    culture, Germany
    Stankowski + Duschek, Germany, 1992
    Stylized floral motif for a horticultural exhibition in
    the Bavarian town of Ingolstadt.
10. **Quijotesancho** tourism, Spain
    Cruz más Cruz, Spain, 2008
    The simple forms of this modern symbol promote
    'the land of *Don Quijote*' and suggest the book's
    central characters (Don Quijote on the left and
    Sancho Panza on the right).

11. **Stara Planina** timber, Bulgaria
    Sotir Sotirov, Bulgaria, 1971
    Triangular mark reflecting the meaning of
    planina (mountain).

11.

12.

13.

12. Radio El Pais broadcasting, Spain
Cruz más Cruz, Spain, 1984
Strong geometric relationships define the symbol
for a group of Spanish radio stations.

13. Recycling Plant, Sofia recycling, Bulgaria
Stefan Kanchev, Bulgaria, c.1960s–70s
Symbol suggesting the breaking down and
reforming of waste materials.

14. Merck pharmaceuticals, USA
Chermayeff & Geismar, USA, 1991
This leading pharmaceutical company markets
its products worldwide but, because of a name
conflict, it could not use the Merck name in most
European countries. To ensure consistency
across the brand, this bold symbol was combined
with the Merck name in the USA, and with other
names in European markets.

15. Bank of Taipei finance, Taiwan/Taipei
Chermayeff & Geismar, USA, 2009
An abstracted flower with four petals, this
bold form and square evoke security, protection
and trust.

16. Circle Court retail, USA
Unimark International, USA, c.1970s
Symbol echoing the architectural structure and
name of an urban retail development in Chicago.

17. Yale School of Management education, USA
Pentagram, USA, 2008
Symbol for the prestigious graduate school of
business at Yale University.

18. Ameritone Paint Corp manufacturing, USA
Gould & Associates, USA, 1970
Symbol suggesting the range of paints made
by a leading American brand.

19. Noches Blancas Europa events, Spain
Cruz más Cruz, Spain, 2006
Striking symbol hinting at night and day,
designed for a series of 'white night' cultural
events throughout Europe.

20. Laboratori Cosmochimici chemicals, Italy
Walter Ballmer, Italy, date unknown
An appropriately scientific tone is set by the mark
designed for a chemical laboratory.

21. Murkette Company manufacturing, USA
The Design Partnership, USA, 1960
Symbol for a manufacturer of chemicals
and plastics.

22. Kunsten.nu arts and culture, Denmark
Designbolaget, Denmark, 2008
A vibrant 3-D mark for an art forum with online
and offline applications.

23. Public Guardianship government, UK
HGV Pierre Vermeir, UK, 1999
The tree reflects protection and guardianship,
while the pie chart communicates the financial
management on offer to those who lack capacity
within the framework of the Mental Capacity
Act 2005.

24. Space Genie retail, UK
Bibliothèque, UK, 2006
Symbol reflecting the flexibility of a household
storage system produced by this MFI sub-brand.

25. Dayton Hudson retail, USA
Unimark International, USA, c.1970s
Symbol for a retail corporation responsible for
Target, the American supermarket brand. Dayton
Hudson was formed when Dayton acquired the
J.L. Hudson department-store chain in 1969.

14.

15.

16.

17.

18.

19.

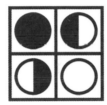

20.

21.

22.

23.

24.

25.

1.

2.

1. **Format** publishing/advertising, Poland
   Karol Sliwka, Poland, 1989
   A white rhombus within a larger black rhombus
   suggests the integrated service provided by an
   agency dealing in both advertising and publishing.
2. **Stadt Weiden in der Oberpfalz**
   tourism, Germany
   Uwe Loesch, Germany, 2002
   The rhombi reference the traditional roof shape
   in the historic city of Weiden, and also recall the
   Bavarian flag.

3. **Puerta de Europa** property development, Spain
   Cruz más Cruz, Spain, 1994
   This symbol echoes the leaning architecture of
   Madrid's 'twin towers', the gateway to the city's
   business district.

4. ***Space Magazine*** publishing, USA
   Julia Hoffmann, USA, 2002
   Symbol for a magazine concerned with personal
   and public space, a project at the School of Visual
   Arts in New York.

3.

4.

BAM (Royal BAM Group nv)

Construction, The Netherlands
Total Identity, The Netherlands, 1999

The Royal BAM Group nv is a 'European construction enterprise' headquartered in Bunnik, near Utrecht in the heart of The Netherlands. Founded in 1869 as a simple carpentry shop, Koninklijke BAM Groep (literally, Royal BAM Group) is the market leader in The Netherlands and now ranks as one of Europes's largest construction groups, with activities in numerous countries worldwide. The concrete columns that provide the foundations of this distinctive symbol provide more than a clue to the nature of this hugely successful business.

Originally designed for BAM NBM by Total Design in 1999, the symbol and accompanying identity were refreshed in 2003 by Total Identity – effectively the same design company. (Founded in 1963 by a group of legendary designers including the likes of Wim Crouwel and Ben Bos, Total Design became Total Identity in 2000.) This distinctly architectural symbol communicates the cohesion of a group comprising numerous companies, while also suggesting the built environment.

Following the 2002 acquisition of HBG (Hollandsche Beton Groep), BAM felt it was important to celebrate the heritage of its latest and largest addition. In 2008, HBG relaunched under the BAM name and identity. BAM acknowledged the history of its new acquisition by incorporating its colour palette of orange and green into the BAM identity.

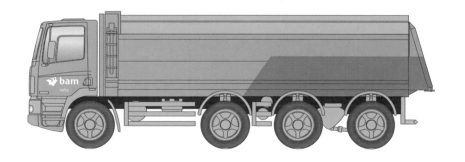

1.

2.

3.

4.

5.

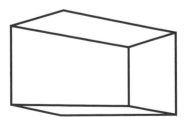

6.

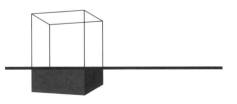

7.

8.

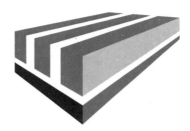

9.

10.

1. **Contena** arts and culture, Japan
   Good Design Company, Japan, 2001
   Mark for an agency representing writers.
2. **Metal Mouldings and Processing Commitee**
   manufacturing, Bulgaria
   Stefan Kanchev, Bulgaria, c.1960s–70s
   A simple cutaway transforms a cube,
   suggesting molten metal being poured
   into a mould.
3. **Alexander Laljak** photography, Germany
   Brand New History, Germany, 2006
   The symbol for a Berlin-based photographer
   recalls the closing aperture of a camera lens.

4. **Bank of Yokohama** finance, Japan
   Interbrand, international, 2007
   Designed for one of Japan's strongest regional
   banks, this symbol is quintessentially Yokohama,
   carrying customers 'toward their dreams'.
   The facing sails express the bank's willingness
   to listen.
5. **Form** hospitality, UK
   Accept & Proceed, UK, 2003
   Symbol for a members-only bar, hinting at the
   secret space to be enjoyed once access
   is granted.
6. **Ryan Associates** construction, USA
   Elixir Design, USA, 2002
   A firmly embedded 3-D mark for a successful
   construction contractor.

7. **System Trans** removals, Germany
   28 Limited Brand, Germany, 2009
   A simple, 3-D form implies motion and the journey
   from an old home to a new one.
8. **Banagher Concrete** construction, Ireland
   Dara Creative, Ireland, 2006
   A suitably sturdy, dependable mark recalls the
   product made by this leading precast-concrete
   specialist.
9. **Treuerevision GmbH** consultancy, Germany
   Büro Uebele Visuelle Kommunikation, Germany, 2001
   The rays of a 'star' suggest a dynamic company,
   the two directions reflecting its proactive and
   reactive aspects.
10. **AR/WO X** community initiatives, Austria
    Buero X Vienna, Austria, 1997
    Mark symbolizing the fusion of working and living
    spaces for an organization aimed at young
    entrepreneurs.

11.

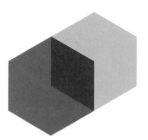

12.

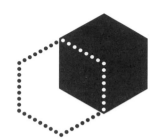

13.

14.

15.

16.

17.

18.

19.

20.

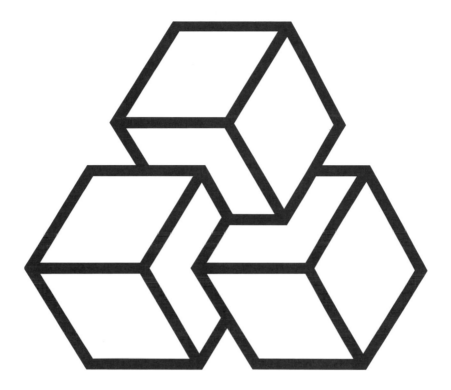

11. **Relate** business support, Denmark
re-public, Denmark, 2007
Two cubes interact to reflect an efficient business using digital media to build client audience relationships.

12. **Tietoa Finland Ltd.**
architecture/engineering, Finland
Hahmo, Finland, 2008
Company providing computer-based BIM (Building Information Modelling) services for the construction industry.

13. **rosamax** interior design, Germany
Pascal Rohé/seventysix, Germany, 2003
A fragmented cube implies the architectural spaces brought to life by the client.

14. **Espace Paul Wurth** arts and culture, Luxembourg
Vidale Gloesner, Luxembourg, 2007
A 3-D box represents space in this symbol for a temporary art gallery opened as part of Luxembourg's 2007 European City of Culture festivities.

15. **GoldCore** finance, Ireland
Creative Inc., Ireland, 2008
A literal translation of the company name; the cube within a cube suggests security.

16. **Packpacka** packaging, Ukraine
Headshot brand development, Ukraine, 2008
A 3-D object implies the business of an online packaging resource.

17. **Statens Informasjonstjeneste: auditing**
government, Norway
Paul Brand, Norway, 1968
A strong mark suggesting the integrity of an organization responsible for auditing and controlling government accounts.

18. **The Point** property development, UK
Clusta, UK, 2007
Distinctive architectural forms create a modern mark that communicates integrity and innovation.

19. **Nederlandse Museumvereniging**
arts and culture, The Netherlands
Edenspiekermann, The Netherlands, 2003
Symbol for a museum card granting the holder discounted access to over 400 museums. Commissioned by The Netherlands Museum Association.

20. **Banco de Estado do Rio Grande do Sul**
finance, Brazil
Aloisio Magalhães Programação Visual Desenho Industrial Ltda, Brazil, date unknown
A strong image for a Rio de Janeiro bank.

The Cooper Union

Education, USA
Doyle Partners, USA, 2009

Established in 1859, the Cooper Union for the Advancement of Science and Art is among the USA's oldest and most distinguished institutions of higher learning. From the very beginning, the Cooper Union has exuded a distinctly philanthropic air, providing a public reading room and playing host to a distinguished list of speakers including social and political reformers, and several future US presidents, among them Abraham Lincoln, William Howard Taft, Theodore Roosevelt and Barack Obama. Through academic programmes in art, architecture and engineering, the Cooper Union 'prepares talented students to make enlightened contributions to society'. With a new academic building rising on Cooper Square and a 150th anniversary just around the corner, it was decided that a new identity could, in the words of Stephen Doyle, who was invited to design it, 'graphically signal Cooper's vitality, its complexity, its energy and its unity'.

Doyle drew on his own experiences at Cooper as student, teacher, and subsequently a trustee. Cooper's president, Dr George Campbell, believed the symbol should 'transcend history, tradition and culture, and embrace the future'. Doyle wanted it to suggest art and science, as well as their union, and his solution is rooted in logic.

'If you draw a C or a U as a square form,' he says, 'you arrive at our basic module: three planes that intersect at right angles. If you twist the U one rotation, its three planes complement the three planes of the C, creating a perfect square, an ideal geometric form useful in engineering, art and architecture. We allowed our planes to intersect just at their points, encouraging them to be transparent.'

The three primary colours were selected because they are 'the genesis of all colours'. It is a visual palette that instils the new Cooper Union identity with a celebratory spirit: a thoroughly modern symbol driven by notions of creative and scientific endeavour.

21.

22.

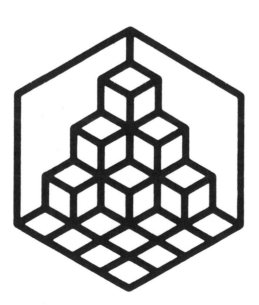

23.

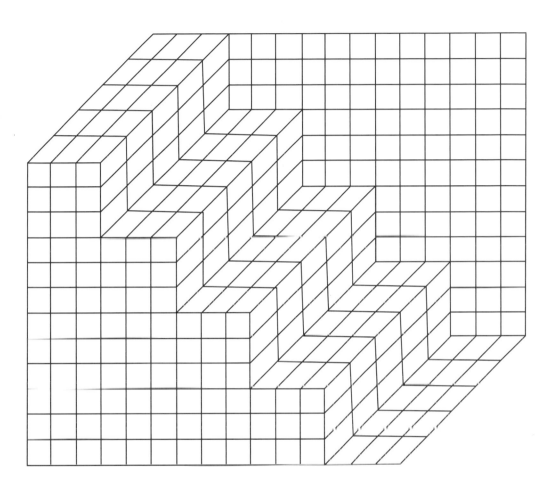

21. International Crane Conference
construction, USA
Essex Two, USA, date unknown
Symbol commissioned by Clark Equipment
Company, a manufacturer of industrial and
construction machinery.

22. L'Escalier fashion, Italy
Michele Spera, Italy, 1970
A 3-D cube gives way to the stairs of the fashion
brand's name.

23. Buro Happold engineering, UK
Pentagram, UK, 1977
An evocative and distinctly architectural mark
for an international structural engineering firm.

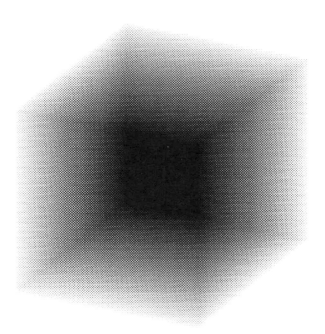

Museum für Gegenwartskunst Siegen

Arts and culture, Germany
Uwe Loesch, Germany, 2001

The founding principle of the Museum für Gegenwartskunst Siegen is, rather appropriately, the 'exploration of the interaction between art and communication technologies'. Appropriate because the museum occupies a former municipal telegraph building acquired in the late 1990s by the city of Siegen, east of Cologne. Modified by German architect Josef P. Kleihues (1933–2004), the gallery offers 1700m^2 (18,298 ft^2) of space devoted to work that explores the interaction of art and new media since the early twentieth century. Tasked with designing an identity for this new and innovative museum, Uwe Loesch – one of Germany's leading designers and design professors – set about embodying the museum's unique mission and spirit.

Launched in 2000 to promote the new museum (which opened its doors to the public the following year), Loesch's identity was driven by a distinct and unusual symbol: a monochromatic square shifted 11 degrees to create a parallelogram and extended to create an ethereal, shape-shifting cube. Appearing alternately in black on white and white on black, it was truly a symbol of the digital age.

Though just as effective in print as it is on-screen, Loesch's symbol really came to life when animated, rotating both clockwise and anticlockwise, shifting between two and three dimensions. A loop of this animation could be seen on a large outdoor screen above the entrance to the building, symbolizing the museum's personality as well as its mission to celebrate the interaction of art and new media. The identity designed by Loesch was retained until the end of 2004 when, rather appropriately, it evolved. The original symbol was retained, however, albeit it on a slightly smaller scale.

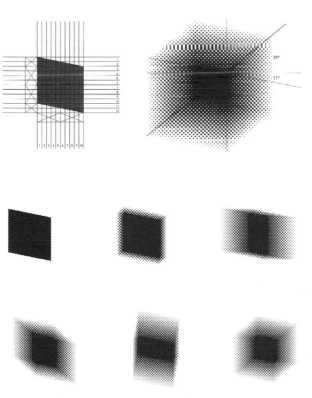

Eröffnung 6. Mai 2001

Museum für Gegenwartskunst Siegen

1.

2.

3.

4.

5.

1. **60I40** arts and culture, UK
   Purpose, UK, 2008
   A confident symbol echoing the name of a group of independent artists committed to bringing applied arts into the 21st century.

2. **The Goldman Warehouse**
   arts and culture, USA
   karlssonwilker, USA, 2006
   An enigmatic statement for a Miami art gallery devoted to private collections of abstract art.

3. **CEER** non-profit organizations, European Union
   Studio FM Milano, Italy, 2001
   Notions of equality are expressed in this bold mark for The Council of European Energy Regulators.

4. **Tucumán** tourism, Argentina
   Bernardo + Celis, Argentina, 2009
   Mark designed to promote tourism in the north-western province of Tucumán. It was designed in collaboration with Estudio Visual Creativo.

5. **Demenz Support Stuttgart GmbH**
   healthcare, Germany
   Büro Uebele Visuelle Kommunikation, Germany, 2003
   This symbol for a company involved in 'transferring knowledge' about dementia recalls the branching out of nerve pathways or the veins of a leaf.

6.

7.

8.

9.

10.

11.

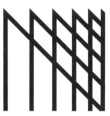

12.

13.

14.

15.

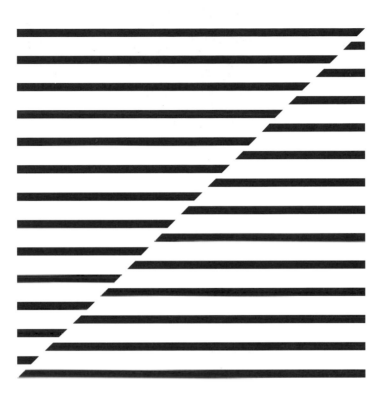

6. **Drukarnia w Oficynie** printing, Poland
Karol Sliwka, Poland, 1988
Symbol suggesting human interaction with paper;
for a high street printer, binder and office supplies
brand.

7. **Zentrum für BrennstoffzellenTechnik** energy,
Germany
Lockstoff Design, Germany, 2002
A progressive tone is set by the symbol for
this centre of fuel-cell technology and research
in Duisburg.

8. **Arnold Schönberg Center** arts and
culture, Austria
*Bohatsch Visual Communication GmbH,
Austria, 1997*
This symbol for a library, archive and gallery
named after the great Austrian composer
aptly hints at musical notation.

9. **Ascot Corp.** property development, Japan
Taku Satoh Design Office Inc., Japan, 2006
An urban skyline reflects the business of a
company specializing in residential properties.

10. **Codarts** education, The Netherlands
75B, The Netherlands, 2005
A modern, sophisticated mark for an arts
university in Rotterdam that specializes in music
and dance.

11. **Stahlhochbau RAL** construction, Germany
Stankowski + Duschek, Germany, 1977
Symbol suggesting the work of a steel structure
construction company.

12. **Ferstenberg-Grunstein**
diamond polishing, Israel
Dan Reisinger, Israel, 1975
Symbol hinting at the facets of a diamond, while
avoiding the visual cliché of a traditional diamond
shape.

13. **Landesmuseum für Technik und Arbeit in
Mannheim** arts and culture, Germany
Stankowski + Duschek, Germany, 1990
Machine-like symbol for the State Museum
of Technology and Work, known today as the
'Technoseum'.

14. **Münchener Rück Ag** insurance, Germany
Stankowski + Duschek, Germany, 1974
A modern mark for a reinsurance business
working in all classes of insurance worldwide.
This symbol is still in use.

15. **Fair Value REIT-AG** property, Germany
Fuenfwerken, Germany, 2008
Symbol conveying the company's ability to
balance vitality and stability.

1.

2.

3.

4.

5.

6.

7.

8.

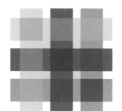

9.

1. **Tokyo Metropolitan University**
   education, Japan
   Taku Satoh Design Office Inc., Japan, 2005
   A simple mark for one of Japan's largest public universities.
2. **Seven Film Gallery** arts and culture, Greece
   Designers United, Greece, 2007
   A chequered motif based on the figure 7.
3. **Columbia Business School** education, USA
   Pentagram, USA, 2007
   Representing the Greek god Hermes, this revitalized version of the school's existing symbol expresses notions of business, commerce and communication.

4. **Burlington Industries** manufacturing, USA
   Chermayeff & Geismar, USA, 1967
   A woven motif suggests both industry and unity for a group of diversified textile-manufacturing companies.
5. **Montiel Craft Center** retail, USA
   John Rieben/Mobium/RR Donnelley, USA, 1990
   Symbol for a specialist in craft and art supplies.
6. **Bernese Orchestral Society**
   music, Switzerland
   Adolf Flückiger, Switzerland, date unknown
   A suitably musical tone is set by this symbol.

7. **United Banks of Colorado** finance, USA
   Chermayeff & Geismar, USA, 1972
   Bold, interlocking motifs suggest strength, security and integrity, important values for a bank to convey.
8. **Infratil** finance, New Zealand
   Cato Partners, Australia, 1997
   Mark symbolizing the layers of a group with businesses in the energy, airport and public transport sectors.
9. **The Green Ribbon Quality Mark** food and beverages, Israel
   Dan Reisinger, Israel, 1964
   Symbol designed to help Israeli consumers to identify quality food and produce.

10.

11.

10. **The Woolmark Company** quality certification, Australia
Francesco Saroglia, Italy, 1964
Encouraging consumer confidence around the world, this iconic symbol was launched in 1964 as a universal endorsement of quality. Inspired by a basic ball of wool, its clarity and simplicity transcend language barriers and negate the need for a logotype. It proved such an influential symbol that the organization responsible for commissioning its design, the Australian-based International Wool Secretariat, changed its name in 1997 to The Woolmark Company. The Woolmark logo is reproduced with the kind permission of Australian Wool Innovation Limited, owner of The Woolmark Company.

11. **Jack Lenor Larson** textiles, USA
Arnold Saks Associates, USA, 1966
This woven mark clearly indicates the business of a leading designer and manufacturer of textiles.

12.

13.

14.

15.

16.

17.

18.

19.

20.

21.

22.

12. National Arts Centre Ottawa
arts and culture, Canada
*Design Collaborative (Ernst Roch and Rolf Harder),
Canada, 1969*
Three intertwined hexagons represent the three
original theatres of the NAC complex, and the
three performing arts disciplines – dance, drama
and music.

13. Genomic Disorders Research Centre medical
research, Australia
Sadgrove Design, Australia, 1998
Symbol recalling the intertwining structure
of a double helix.

14. AIDS Management Standard healthcare,
South Africa
Mister Walker, South Africa, 2004
Two charity ribbons are combined to reflect the
symbol's 'hope is a human resource' strapline.

15. Astral telecoms, Romania
Brandient, Romania, 2003
A looped ribbon motif suggests connectivity for
one of Romania's leading telecoms providers.

16. Ensimbini Terminals logistics, South Africa
Mister Walker, South Africa, 2005
Symbol implying the coming and going of
shipping for South Africa's principal steel export
terminal in Durban harbour.

17. Cultureel Erfgoed Noord-Holland arts and
culture, The Netherlands
Edenspiekermann, The Netherlands, 2007
An infinity symbol for an organization
safeguarding the future of Noord-Holland's
cultural heritage.

18. Assurant insurance, USA
Carbone Smolan Agency, USA, 2003
The motif captures Assurant's unique ability
to integrate a trio of strengths: risk management,
administrative systems and distribution
relationships.

19. POLCOFRA Sp. z o. o. PPH clothing and
accessories, Poland
Karol Sliwka, Poland, 1990
A woven motif indicates the client's tailoring
business.

20. One United Bank finance, USA
BrandEquity, USA, 2000
The knot expresses notions of strength, unity
and value – essential qualities for any banking
institution.

21. Parque de Attraciones de Madrid sport and
leisure, Spain
ruiz+company, Spain, 2004
This playful mark for a theme park recalls the
thrilling experience of riding in a roller coaster.

22. Ahlstrom manufacturing, Finland
Porkka & Kuutsa, Finland, 1999–2000
A fibre tree symbolizes the new and strategic
business operations of a leading global
manufacturer of speciality papers and
non-wovens.

23.

24.

25.

26.

27.

28.

29.

30.

31.

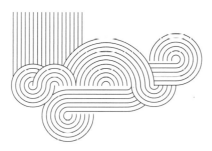

32.

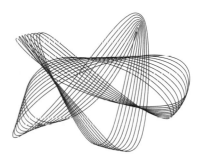

23. Australian Genetic Testing
sports science, Australia
emerystudio, Australia, 2009
A subtle, scientific mark for an organization
providing genetic testing for the horse-racing
industry.

24. Radiocom telecoms, Romania
Brandient, Romania, 2005
The symbol for one of Romania's leading telecoms
brands suggests technology, progress and
communication.

25. Chemia chemicals, Poland
Karol Sliwka, Poland, 1967–68
Symbol for a Polish organization responsible for
the import and export of chemicals.

26. MTA transport, USA
Howard York/YorkBranding, USA, 1974
Mark created for a New York Metropolitan
Transportation Authority promotion encouraging
people to conserve energy by using public
transport. It represents MTA's three main modes
of transport: air, surface and subway.

27. BABCO property development, USA
Essex Two, USA, 1996
A bold, architectural mark for a high-end
contractor specializing in hotels, showrooms
and penthouses.

28. Paslode Tool Company manufacturing, USA
Essex Two, USA, 1985
Symbol designed for a manufacturer of
compressor-driven nailing tools and supplies.

29. First Citizens Bank finance, Trinidad & Tobago
Lippincott, USA, 2005
Interlocking arches communicate energy, growth,
flexibility, partnership and the vibrant multicultural
environment in which the bank operates.

30. Thierry Corde hospitality, USA
Automatic Art and Design, USA, 2007
An intricate, illustrative symbol for an international
luxury spa and pool brand.

31. Corduroy media, Australia
Studio Round, Australia, 2008
A playful cloud motif for an events, PR and
marketing company based in Melbourne.

32. Wagamama restaurants, UK
Pentagram, UK, 1996
A dynamic, noodle-inspired motif is derived
from the star above the oriental restaurant
chain's logotype.

1.

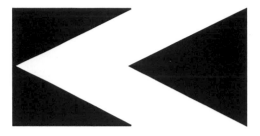

2.

1. **Plate Umzüge** removals, Germany
   Stankowski + Duschek, Germany, 1968
   This mark for a transport and removals company
   conveys the action of moving from one place
   to another.

2. **Fast Take** retail, USA
   Pentagram, USA, 1999
   The mark for an interactive movie-rental kiosk
   recalls the fast-forward symbol.

3. **Citroën** automotive, France
   *André Citroën, France, c.1903; redesigned by
   Landor Associates, international, 2009*
   Working alongside Citroën's designers, Landor
   refreshed this iconic symbol as part of a
   comprehensive identity programme. Embodying
   Citroën's new promise of *créative technologie*, it
   is the most recent update of a symbol originally
   designed by the company's founder André Citroën
   c.1903. The chevron is actually based on a
   herringbone gear, a design that brought great
   success to Citroën's gear-wheel factory.
   The company started making cars in 1919.

4. **Imian** property development, USA
   Arnold Saks Associates, USA, 2006
   A chevron indicates a row of roofed properties.

5. **Spóldzielnia Pracy POWISLE** clothing and
   accessories, Poland
   Karol Sliwka, Poland, 1965
   An appropriate and evocative symbol for a
   manufacturer of uniforms.

6. **Avidia Banking** finance, USA
   BrandEquity, USA, 2007
   This symbol for a Massachusetts bank
   communicates growth and direction.

7. **DW Graham & Associates Ltd** architecture/
   landscape design, Canada
   Georges Beaupré, Canada, 1963
   Symbol for a landscape architect based in Ottawa.

8. **Rossano** property, Argentina
   Bernardo + Celis, Argentina, 2005
   A simple architectural device for a company
   sourcing apartments and suites for
   temporary rental.

9. **Ace Express Group** logistics, Ireland
   Dara Creative, Ireland, 2005
   A dynamic and distinctly modern arrow motif for
   Ireland's leading privately owned and operated
   freight company.

10. **The Aga Khan Fund for Economic
    Development** economic development, USA
    Pentagram, UK, 1986
    The bar-chart element depicts growth, while the
    woven positive/negative elements reflect
    interdependence between developed and
    developing worlds.

11. **CIS Bio International** biomedical, France
    Rudi Meyer/Sherpa, France, 1987
    An organic tone distinguishes the mark designed
    for this biomedical firm, part of Groupe Oris.

3.

4.

5.

6.

7.

8.

9.

10.

11.

1.

2.

3.

4.

5.

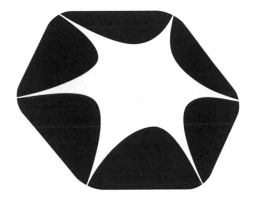

6.

1. **Mitsubishi Motors Corporation**
    automotive, Japan
    Yataro Iwasaki, Japan, 1870
    Virtually unchanged for 140 years, the visual form
    derives from *mitsu* (three) and *hishi* (water
    chestnut) – the traditional Japanese symbol for
    a diamond shape.

2. **Laverne** interior design, USA
    Arnold Saks Associates, USA, 1967
    Mark suggesting the interior space of a room
    for a manufacturer of modern furniture and wall
    coverings.

3. **Aquamarine** health and beauty, Japan
    Knowledge Plus, Japan, 2004
    An elegant and aspirational diamond formation for
    a leading Japanese perfume brand.

4. **Naceo** Internet, Switzerland
    Bionic Systems, Germany, 2007
    Two forms blend to create a diamond for a web-
    development consultancy based in Geneva.

5. **American Ideal Diamond Corp.** jeweller, USA
    Gabi Toth, Romania, 2003
    A 3-D cut gem suggests a tangible sense of
    luxury.

6. **Majestic** model agency, Argentina
    Design Has No Name (DHNN), Argentina, 2009
    A finely cut diamond reflects the quality service
    and 'rare finds' represented by a Buenos Aires
    model agency.

1.

2.

3.

4.

5.

6.

7.

8.

9.

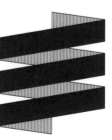

10.

11.

1. **Waser** arts and culture, Austria
    Q2 Design, Austria, 2003
    A subtle motif designed for a crafts enterprise.
2. **BHP** manufacturing, Australia
    Cato Partners, Australia, 2001
    This flag-like symbol indicates progress and
    movement and also suggests the flexibility
    of sheet metal.
3. **Challenge Your World** business development/
    environmental advocacy, Canada
    Method Inc., USA, 2008
    A stylized graph conveys personal growth for
    an organization investing in young people with
    innovative ideas.
4. **Norditalia** insurance, Italy
    Waibl Heinz Studio Signo, Italy, 1986
    An abstract mark sets a solid, dependable tone
    for this Italian insurance company.

5. **Tel Aviv Stock Exchange** finance, Israel
    Dan Reisinger, Israel, 1982
    The repeating motif is based on the peaks
    and troughs of a stock-market graph chart.
6. **UFA** film, Germany
    Buero X Vienna, Austria, 1992
    A new mark for one of cinema's most historic
    companies: Universum Film AG.
7. **Silverstone** sport and leisure, UK
    Carter Wong Design, UK, 2002
    This proud, patriotic mark for the home of
    British motor sports captures the speed and
    excitement of racing.
8. **Ingenieurbau-Preis** publishing, Germany
    Stankowski + Duschek, Germany, 1988
    Symbol for an imprint of Ernst & Sohn specializing
    in construction engineering and architecture.
    The symbol is still in use.

9. **London Restaurant Festival** events, UK
    NB: Studio, UK, 2009
    This symbol for a festival celebrating London's
    diverse range of restaurants was inspired by
    the excitement, collective optimism and visual
    aesthetic of the 1951 Festival of Britain.
10. **Breast Cancer Care** charity, UK
    Spencer du Bois, UK, 2008
    An evolved ribbon with stripes distinguishes
    the client from charities who have adopted the
    generic pink ribbon.
11. **Marca País Argentina** tourism, Argentina
    Cabina, Argentina, 2005
    Patriotic colours and a celebratory spirit define
    the symbol that promotes tourism in Argentina.

1.

2.

3.

4.

5.

6.

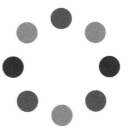

1. **Amango.de** media, Germany
   Tisch Eins, Germany, 2004
   A simple image of a disc communicates the
   service provided by this online DVD rental service.
2. **Hyatt Place** hospitality, USA
   Lippincott, USA, 2005
   The regularly arranged circles in this friendly,
   modern symbol supports the idea of the hotel
   as a gathering place.

3. **intercell** biotechnology, Austria
   Alessandri Design, Austria, 2002
   Intercell develops vaccines for the prevention and
   treatment of infectious diseases.
4. **Butina** manufacturing, Denmark
   Punktum Design, Denmark, 2003
   Abstract mark for Denmark's leading supplier of
   integrated systems for the humane handling of
   pigs in abattoirs.

5. **Tschiesche Architekten** architecture, Germany
   *Büro Uebele Visuelle Kommunikation,
   Germany, 1997*
   The dots that make up this symbol reflect the
   practice's work with modular structures that
   always use a matrix.
6. **Performance Collision Center** automotive, USA
   Lodge Design, USA, 2008
   The loop suggests efficiency and a speedy
   turnaround, reflecting the company's
   state-of-the-art facilities.

7.

8.

9.

10.

11.

12.

7. **Breaking the Ice** non-profit organizations, Germany
    Pentagram, Germany, 2002
    The client's mission to foster trust and mutual respect between conflicting peoples is reflected in this symbol.

8. **GEI** education, Switzerland
    Vingtneuf degres sàrl, Switzerland, 2006
    Mark conveying technology and innovation for an agricultural institute in Fribourg, western Switzerland.

9. **Pepper** media, UK
    Fivefootsix, UK, 2005
    This symbol adopts the familiar holes at the top of a pepper pot for this post-production company.

10. **Private Brauereien Bayern e.V.** professional association, Germany
    KMS TEAM, Germany, 2006
    The bubbles found in beer are captured to form a classic star suggesting excellence.

11. **Pillsbury & Company 'Made For Microwave'** food and beverages, USA
    Essex Two, USA, 1984
    Mark designed for a sub-brand specializing in food for microwave cooking.

12. **Indra** information technology, Spain
    Saffron Brand Consultants, UK, 2007
    An existing symbol was developed, maintaining the essence of an innovative company with an international scope.

13.

14.

15.

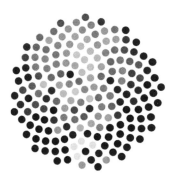

16.

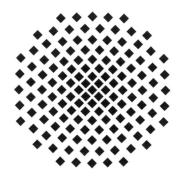

13. Sydney Eye Specialist Centre healthcare, Australia
North Design & Branding, Australia, 2006
Avoiding clichés, this symbol suggests the scientific cutting edge offered by a Sydney ophthalmic practice.

14. Everbrite Electric Signs Inc.
manufacturing, USA
George Nelson & Company, USA, 1963
Radiating dots illustrate the idea of light in this symbol for a manufacturer of electric signs.

15. Seed Media Group publishing, USA
Sagmeister Inc., USA, 2005
A versatile symbol based on phyllotaxis – the arrangement of leaves on a plant stem – for a publisher of science magazines, books and films.

16. Universität Stuttgart education, Germany
Stankowski + Duschek, Germany, 1987
The mark for Stuttgart's historic university suggests notions of technology, innovation and the dissemination of knowledge. The symbol is still in use.

17. Sunrise Consultants property, Belgium/USA
Chilli Design & Multimedia, Belgium, 2009
A friendly sun motif designed to attract Belgians to the prospect of owning real estate in Florida.

18. Grafika Publishing Internet, Germany
Toman Graphic Design, Czech Republic, 2003
Layered dots stretch around a globe to convey the digital and international nature of the client's business.

19. Weltholz timber, Germany
KMS TEAM, Germany, 2009
A globe consisting of timber samples symbolizes Weltholz's worldwide importing activities.

20. GotSpot technology, UK
Fivefootsix, UK, 2007
Symbol designed to be used in isolation from the logotype as an identifier of wireless connectivity.

21. Energy Australia energy, Australia
Cato Partners, Australia, 1995
Mark for a leading electricity retailer suggesting an illuminated city and an energy grid at work.

22. Paramount hospitality, UK
Mind Design, UK, 2008
Symbol for a members' club and restaurant at the top of Centre Point in London; it is constructed from 33 elements, one for each floor.

17.

18.

19.

20.

21.

22.

1.

2.

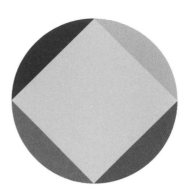

3.

4.

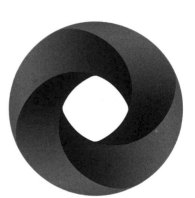

5.

6.

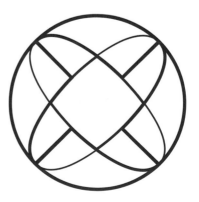

7.

8.

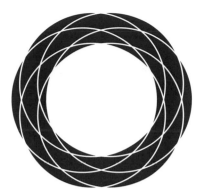

9.

1. **Circulo de Lectores** retail, Spain
   Interbrand, international, 2006
   A painterly mark injects a sense of vibrancy
   and creativity into this Spanish bookstore chain.
2. **International Olympic Congress** international
   relations/sport and leisure, Germany
   Stankowski + Duschek, Germany, 1981
   Each segment of this stylized ring features a
   colour from the original Olympic logo: red, blue,
   yellow and green.
3. **Green Employer Council** employment, USA
   Addis Creson, USA, 2008
   Designed for an organization that helps people
   to progress through training to internships and
   jobs, this symbol represents membership, pride
   and unity.

4. **Grant Thornton** consultancy/finance, UK
   Pentagram, UK, 2007
   Symbol for a global accountancy and consultancy
   firm draws inspiration from a Möbius strip to
   represent permanence, consistency and flexibility.
5. **Kristy Harrison** photography, Canada
   Rethink Communications, Canada, 2008
   A distinctive symbol that identifies the client as
   a leader within the specialized area of wedding
   photography.
6. **Igalia** engineering, Spain
   38one, USA, 2005–06
   A mark for an engineering company whose
   main objective is to develop solutions based
   on free software.

7. **SULL** healthcare, UK
   Cartlidge Levene, UK, 2005
   A secure ring motif for a pioneering medical
   product enabling doctors to safely attach
   medical tubes to patients.
8. **Central Presentations** media, UK
   Slingshot, UK, 2002
   A camera lens seen at an angle suggests
   the energy and drive of this audio-visual
   production company.
9. **BitStreams** events, USA
   Pentagram, USA, 2002
   Symbol for an exhibition of interactive and
   technology-driven art; it was commissioned
   by one of the exhibition sponsors, Zurich
   Capital Markets.

1.

2.

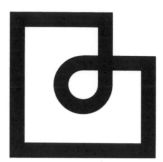

3.

1. **Promaint** infrastructure, Finland
Hahmo, Finland, 2008
A modern, professional image for an infrastructure/maintenance group seeking to increase Finnish productivity; the infinity symbol also suggests a conveyor belt.

2. **Complejo Plastico Isla Margarita**
tourism, Venezuela
Nedo Mion Ferrario, Venezuela, 1970
Symbol for a holiday village for artists; this creative mark was perhaps inspired by an artist's palette.

3. **Double Knot** film, UK
Stylo, UK/France, 2004
A bold, symmetrical interpretation of the film production company's name.

4. **Biomedical Simulation Centre** biomedical, Portugal
Bürocratik, Portugal, 2008
Symbol for a medical research centre exploring the possibilities of technological developments in healthcare.

5. **Tomono Agrica** chemicals, Japan
Katsuichi Ito Design Office, Japan, 1993
Mark symbolizing the coming together of agriculture and science.

6. **Charter Club, Macy's** fashion, USA
Wink, Incorporated, USA, 2005
Elegant symbol for Macy's in-store, upmarket private-label brand.

7. **Carborundum** abrasives, USA
A. Richard de Natale, USA, date unknown
A smooth form suggests the effect of using abrasives – industrial materials, often minerals, used to shape or finish a range of products.

8. **Japan Nuclear Fuel Limited** energy, Japan
Katsuichi Ito Design Office, Japan, 1992
Symbol reflecting the innovative technologies employed by a company that reprocesses nuclear fuel waste.

9. **Vedfelt Instituttet** education, Denmark
Applied Projects, Denmark, 2009
Mark for an institute dealing with cybernetic psychology – the study of the structure of complex systems.

10. **Bennett Schneider** retail, USA
Design Ranch, USA, 2006
An elegant, crafted symbol supports the high-quality stationery on sale at this store in Kansas City, Missouri.

11. **Luto** pharmaceuticals, UK
The One Off, UK, 2008
A stylized eye communicates notions of clarity and warmth for a company specializing in enhancing communication to patients and healthcare professionals.

12. **SACD, Scam and Sofam** professional association, Belgium
Coast, Belgium, 2008
A dynamic guilloche for a group of three societies representing the rights and work of writers and artists.

4.

5.

6.

7.

0.

9.

10.

11.

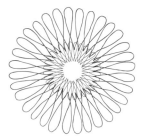

12.

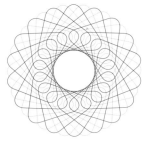

1.

2.

3.

4.

5.

6.

7.

8.

9.

1. **WDA (Workforce Development Agency)** government, UK
   Funnel Creative, UK, 2008
   A graphic learning curve reflects the positive effort required to acquire new skills.
2. **Fair Play** sport and leisure, Germany
   Stankowski + Duschek, Germany, 1986
   Two simple curves hint at myriad sports; the symbol was designed for a German sports initiative.

3. **Detaillisten Sempach** professional associations, Switzerland
   Erich Brechbühl (Mixer), Switzerland, 2002
   Symbol suggesting collaboration for a retailers' federation in the Swiss town of Sempach.
4. **The Australian Ballet** arts and culture, Australia
   3 Deep Design, Australia, 2006
   Dancing figures represent the blend of tradition and innovation offered by one of Australia's flagship arts companies.

5. **Scanteam** media/technology, Belgium
   Chilli Design & Multimedia, Belgium, 2006
   A human eye represents a company specializing in scanning company archives for online and offline access.
6. **Thai Airlines** transport, global
   Interbrand, International, 2005
   Symbol inspired by the 'jumpee' symbol, the traditional 'wai' greeting of bringing the two palms together and the pitched roof of Thai architecture.

10.

11.

7. **Motoring** sport and leisure, Poland
Karol Sliwka, Poland, 1994
A symbol reflecting the energy and speed
of motor sports.

8. **Dura Vermeer** engineering, The Netherlands
Teldesign, The Netherlands, 2000
Evocative mark suggesting roads for one of
The Netherlands' leading construction and
development groups.

9. **Baiyun Airport** transport, China
Cato Partners, Australia, 2004
This symbol for a Chinese airport reflects its
graceful architecture and the idea of travel.

10. **S-IG** technology, Argentina
Bernardo + Celis, Argentina, 2005
A dynamic symbol suggesting connectivity
and progress.

11. **BührmannUbbens** paper, The Netherlands
Teldesign, The Netherlands, 2003
Distinctive symbol for a Dutch market leader
in paper, envelopes and packaging supplies.

Continental Airlines

Transport, USA
Saul Bass, USA, 1968 (shown here);
since modified by Lippincott Mercer, USA, 1991

Founded in 1934 in Texas, Varney Speed Lines operated airmail and passenger services in the American Southwest. In 1937 the company changed its name to Continental Airlines, in line with its expanding network and the desire of Robert F. Six (Continental Airlines' legendary CEO between 1936 and 1981) to have the airline fly to destinations throughout North America.

The current Continental Airlines symbol – a cropped blue globe framed by a blue square – suggests the dynamism and scope of international air travel. Designed in 1991 by Lippincott Mercer, it reflects the fact that Continental Airlines has become one of the world's most widely travelling airlines, flying to destinations throughout the USA, Canada, Latin America, Europe and the Asia-Pacific regions.

The current identity succeeded one of air travel's most iconic identities, the simplified jet-stream symbol designed in 1968 by Saul Bass (1920–96). Commissioned to design a new mark and livery, Bass created a bold and dynamic symbol, reflecting the modern values of a growing and progressive airline. The design also took into consideration Six's plan to fly to destinations in the Pacific Far East within five years. The symbol was applied in a number of colours, including red, black, white and gold, with the colour changing to suit specific applications. The most frequently used colour was red; originally black, the tail-fin symbol changed to red around a decade after the original programme rolled out. This design programme was, at the time, one of the most comprehensive in the USA, encompassing over 400 applications from plane liveries, vehicles and uniforms to baggage tags, cutlery, air-sickness bags and blankets.

The authors would like to reiterate that the symbol featured on these pages is not the symbol currently used by Continental Airlines. We would like to thank them for allowing us to include their previous identity in this book.

12.

13.

14.

15.

I6.

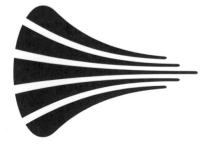

17.

18.

19.

20.

21.

12. Instituto Nacional de Promoción Turística tourism, Argentina
Estudio Soma, Argentina, 2009
A celebratory, birdlike mark promoting tourism in Argentina.

13. IAG insurance, New Zealand
Cato Partners, Australia, 1997
IAG is an international insurance group with operations in Australia, New Zealand, the UK and Asia.

14. Qlicks marketing, The Netherlands
unieq, The Netherlands, 2008
Symbol for an online marketing company; the three 'qlicks' represent clicks on a mouse button.

15. National Museum of Nature and Science arts and culture, Japan
Taku Satoh Design Office Inc., Japan, 2007
An ambiguous rhythmic parabola supports the museum's motto: 'Explore the Power of Imagination'.

16. Sysmex Corporation manufacturing, Japan
Ken Miki & Associates, Japan, 1998
Symbol for a manufacturer of laboratory equipment and automated analyzers based in Kobe, Japan.

17. Dayton retail, USA
Unimark International, USA, c.1965–69
Symbol for a leading American retail group that became Dayton Hudson in 1969.

18. Department Store retail, Bulgaria
Stefan Kanchev, Bulgaria, c.1960s–70s
An elegant architectural motif for a department store in Sofia.

19. Fenchurch fashion, UK
Slingshot, UK, 2000
Playing on the brand name, this symbol draws on ecclesiastical imagery.

20. ASINCAR engineering, Spain
Zorraquino, Spain, 2005
Geometric curves converge in one direction, expressing technology and strength through unity.

21. CIM energy, France
Rudi Meyer/Sherpa, France, 1990
Symbol for a company formed in 1920 to finance and manage facilities for the reception, storage and transfer of oil products at Le Havre.

Nike

Clothing and accessories, USA
Carolyn Davidson, USA, 1971; modified 1981

The genesis of Nike's Swoosh symbol has gone down in trademark folklore. Carolyn Davidson was a graphic-design student at Portland State University, Oregon, when she first met Phil Knight, the future Nike CEO, who was teaching accountancy classes. Knight's company, Blue Ribbon Sports, was preparing to launch a range of athletic footwear and, having seen her sketching in PSU's corridors, he asked Davidson if she would like to submit some logo ideas for the new line. They agreed on a fee of $2 per hour – not bad for a graphics student in 1971 – and in June of that year she presented her ideas. Knight and his colleagues settled on the Swoosh design, which was based on the wings of Nike, the Greek Goddess of Victory. Davidson invoiced Knight for $35, which he duly paid and that, as they say, was that.

Except it wasn't. Registered as a trademark by Nike, Inc. on 31 January 1972, Davidson's Swoosh has been modified only once; a refreshed version, the one in use today, was registered in March 1981. Today, Nike is a household name; the world's leading supplier of athletic shoes and apparel, it employs some 30,000 people worldwide. Interestingly, the consistency and clarity with which the Nike Swoosh is implemented has negated the need for a logotype; after all, this is a symbol so successful that it has its own name – the Swoosh.

Incidentally, Davidson ended up making more than $35 for her work, when Knight rewarded her in 1983 with a gold ring and an envelope full of Nike stock. Not bad for a student project...

1.

2.

3.

4.

5.

6.

7.

8.

9.

10.

11.

1. **Verbal Communication** public relations, UK
    Clusta, UK, 2005
    A graphic translation of the client's business
    and name.
2. **Architecture & Public Works Committee**
    professional organization, Bulgaria
    Stefan Kanchev, Bulgaria, c.1960s–70s
    A strong mark suggesting notions of construction
    and machinery.
3. **Silex Solar** energy, Australia
    North Design & Branding, Australia, 2009
    The panels reference the solar panels
    manufactured by the client.
4. **Bardmoor Realty** property, USA
    Joseph Bottoni, USA, 1969
    A vibrant, radiating sun sets a positive tone
    for this Florida real-estate agency.

5. **Centrum Onkologii im. Marii
    Sklodowskiej-Curie** healthcare, Poland
    Karol Sliwka, Poland, 2001
    A bright solar symbol designed for an
    oncological research facility.
6. **Kinyo** textiles, Japan
    Yusaku Kamekura, Japan, 1964
    Symbol for a textile wholesaler.
7. **Austro-Chematon** science, Austria
    Erich Buchegger, Austria, date unknown
    A spark of inspiration for a scientific laboratory.
8. **Balkan Film Festival, 1965** events/film, Bulgaria
    Stefan Kanchev, Bulgaria, 1965
    Dynamic symbol recalling the beams of light
    expelled by film projectors.

9. **Huawei** telecoms, China
    Interbrand, international, 2006
    Symbol for a provider of telecommunication
    network solutions to operators around the world;
    Huawei is one of the leading companies in its field.
10. **Rat für Formgebung** arts and culture, Germany
    Stankowski + Duschek, Germany, 1960
    Symbol for the German Design Council founded
    in 1953 to inform the business community about
    the power of design; it is still in use.
11. **Escuela Superior de Diseño Gráfico**
    education, Spain
    El Paso, Galería de Comunicación, Spain, 2005
    A ring of exclamation marks reflects the
    creative processes that take place at this
    graphic-design school.

12.

13.

14.

15.

16.

17.

12. Regenesis Power energy, USA
Hughes design/communications, USA, 2006
The rays of the sun combine with an 'on'
switch for a company supplying renewable
solar energy solutions.

13. Bendigo College of Advanced Education
education, Australia
Sadgrove Design, Australia, 1980
Dynamic mark suggesting intelligence and
innovation for a college that has since merged
with La Trobe University.

14. Gemma jeweller, Ukraine
Artemov Artel, Ukraine, 2007
A stylized interpretation of highly crafted jewels
and the many facets of the client's business.

15. The Danish Arts Council arts and culture,
Denmark
e-Types, Denmark, 2007
An optimistic mark for an organization promoting
artistic development in Denmark and Danish
art abroad.

16. California Academy of Sciences science, USA
Pentagram, USA, 2007
This science institution houses a museum,
planetarium and aquarium.

17. Ciaran O'Flynn jeweller, Ireland
Area, Ireland, 2009
An aspirational mark expressing the radiant
qualities of finely crafted jewellery.

18.

19.

20.

21.

22.

23.

18. Rocky Mountain States tourism, USA
Unimark International, USA, c.1970s
Symbol promoting tourism in the Rocky
Mountain states in western North America.

19. Santa Fe Savings finance, USA
Ken Parkhurst, USA, 1975
The symbol for this savings and loan institution in
America's Southwest recalls the region's Native
American culture.

20. Gorrissen Federspiel legal, Denmark
Saffron Brand Consultants, UK, 2009
Symbol representing teamwork; the emanating
lines derive from names of the firm's partners
and staff.

21. San Francisco Opera arts and culture/music,
USA
Pentagram, USA, 2006
A dynamic symbol suggesting the music
performed by the second largest opera company
in North America.

22. Restauro del Vescovado construction, Italy
KMstudio, Italy, 2000
An elegant mark for a restoration project/
development in the town of Vescovado
near Siena.

23. Protestante Kerk Nederland religion,
The Netherlands
Total Identity Amsterdam bv, The Netherlands, 2004
A dove and helios motif combine to form a cross
in a vibrant, modern identity for the Dutch
Protestant Church.

Munich Olympics 1972

Sport, Germany
Otl Aicher and Coordt von Mannstein, Germany, c.1971–72

When Munich was awarded the 1972 Olympics, it was regarded as an ideal opportunity to overwrite the memory of Germany's last summer games – the 1936 Berlin Games presided over by Hitler. Unfortunately, the killing of 11 Israeli athletes by Palestinian terrorists drew a tragic veil over the Munich Olympics, but in the lead-up to the games every effort was made to define them as the 'happy games', or the 'rainbow games'.

Graphic designers will no doubt be aware of the contribution made by German design legend Otl Aicher – his system of sports pictograms are still used today and his influence is apparent in the vast swathe of printed material, signage and merchandise produced for the games. He led a large team of designers and was hugely passionate about the project's potential, so it must have been a shock when his proposed symbol, a radiating sun motif, was rejected. Despite its later adoption by the German Lottery, Aicher's symbol was deemed impossible to copyright and so the design was put out to competition.

Aicher sat on the panel of judges tasked with finding a winning design, selecting Coordt von Mannstein's proposal. A designer at Graphic Team Cologne, von Mannstein literally put a twist on Aicher's original mark, celebrating the dynamism of sport and athletes with an energetic spiral that recalls diagrams of the Fibonacci sequence. Aicher is often credited with the design of what was known as the 'bright sun', but it seems rather fitting that this Olympic symbol was the result of a more collaborative effort.

1.

2.

3.

4.

5.

6.

7.

1. **Steam Music** music, Austria
    Q2 Design, Austria, 2002
    A simple motif suggesting movement, rhythm and the human ear – all appropriate themes for the client.
2. **Avecs** design, The Netherlands
    unieq, The Netherlands, 2008
    An abstract eye suggests attention to detail for a graphic design company specializing in the design and development of Internet applications.
3. **Aegokeros** publishing, Greece
    Espresso Studio, Greece, 2002
    A simple graphic interpretation of the client's name: *Aegokeros* is Greek for Capricorn.

4. **C&T** telecoms, Australia
    Cato Partners, Australia, 2002
    A visual blend of swift, feline agility and cabling; C&T install high-speed telecommunication networks.
5. **Seven Spirits Bay** tourism, Australia
    David Lancashire Design, Australia, 2002
    This symbol for an ecological resort on Aboriginal land in Australia's Northern Territory borrows from indigenous art.

6. **Laboratoire de Cosmétologie Biologique** health and beauty, France
    Gilles Fiszman, France, 1968
    Symbol for a cosmetics brand.
7. **Peacock Bar** hospitality, UK
    Zip Design, UK, 2004
    Evoking the elaborate patterns on a peacock feather in a contemporary manner.

8.

9.

10.

11.

12.

13.

14.

15.

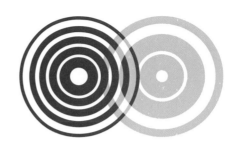

16.

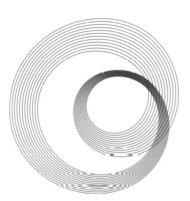

17.

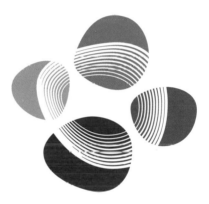

8. **Balarinji** fashion, Australia
Naughtyfish design, Australia, 1999
Aboriginal folk art helps to promote an aspirational and creative fashion-design brand.

9. **EU 2002** government, Denmark
Bysted, Denmark, 2002
Symbol for Denmark's chairmanship of the European Union Commission.

10. **ÖBF** forest administration, Austria
Buero X Vienna, Austria, 1997
The symbol for the Austrian Federal Forests organization uses the concentric rings found in tree trunks.

11. **Dubix** manufacturing, France
Rudi Meyer/dp-industrie, France, 1980
A washing machine in action, this symbol is for a Group Electrolux company that manufactures professional laundry systems.

12. **NetzwerkHolz** professional associations, Germany
KMS TEAM, Germany, 2004
Stylized tree rings symbolize raw materials and growth; the company is part of Klöpferholz GmbH & Co. KG.

13. **Vivien Edwards Homeopathy** healthcare, UK
Cartlidge Levene, UK, 2005
Circles within circles reflect the holistic approach to the alternative medicine practised by the client.

14. **HURDOS** healthcare, Croatia
Likovni Studio, Croatia, 2002
Sound waves touching a child's ear convey the mission of the Croatian Association for Early Hearing Impairment Diagnostics.

15. **Imes Group** engineering, international
Graven Images, UK, 2002
New mark for an international company providing inspection and engineering services to maintain the capability and availability of cranes, lifting equipment and specialized structures.

16. **London Sinfonietta** music, UK
Bibliothèque, UK, 2009
Designed for 'the world's finest contemporary music ensemble', this symbol is a visualization of the sound of a rotary octave.

17. **KAUST** education, Saudi Arabia
Siegel+Gale, USA, 2007
Symbol supporting the motto 'Through inspiration, discovery'; designed for the King Abdullah University of Science and Technology.

1.

2.

1. **Print Irish** printing, Ireland
   Dara Creative, Ireland, 2008
   Symbol designed for a forum promoting print
   and packaging suppliers in Ireland.
2. **Chemelex Corporation** manufacturing, USA
   John Rieben, USA, c.1969
   Symbol for a manufacturer of heat-trace cable for
   frost prevention and assorted electronic devices;
   Chemelex was purchased by Raychem in 1969.
3. **EBS** electronics, Poland
   Karol Sliwka, Poland, 1992
   Electronics company specializing in components
   for car alarms.

4. **NatWest** finance, UK
   *HSAG, UK, 1969; refreshed by The Partners,
   UK, 2001*
   A revitalized version of the iconic NatWest
   symbol, with brighter colours and detailing, lends
   the brand a softer tone. The original was designed
   by HSAG in 1969, following the merger of three
   independent banks – the National, Provincial and
   Westminster. The symbol's geometry is derived
   from three intersecting cubes, which in two
   dimensions also read as three outward-facing
   arrows.
5. **Delta Faucet Company** manufacturing, USA
   Pentagram, USA, 1989
   Manufacturer of domestic and commercial taps.

6. **MINDD Foundation** charity, Australia
   THERE, Australia, 2009
   Symbol supporting MINDD's integrative approach
   to family healthcare, focusing on biomedicine,
   nutrition, neurodevelopment and allied therapies.
7. **Macau Medical Park** healthcare, Ireland
   Area, Ireland, 2008
   A simple, positive mark designed for Sheehan
   Medical, a private hospital operator.
8. **Transammonia** chemicals/transport, USA
   Arnold Saks Associates, USA, 1968
   The symbol for the world's largest ammonia
   shipping company brings to mind the
   journeys involved.

3.

4.

5.

6.

7.

8.

9.

10.

11.

12.

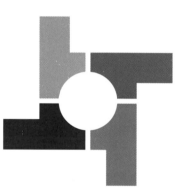

13.

14.

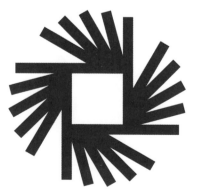

15.

16.

17.

18.

9. **Central National Bank** finance, USA
Unimark International, USA, 1970
An abstract mark for a bank looking to shed its out-of-date image. At the time it was launched such marks were relatively unusual in the banking world.

10. **Taiyo Machine Industry Co.**
manufacturing, Japan
Yusaku Kamekura, Japan, 1958
Rotary symbol for a machine-tool manufacturer suggesting both the process and the end product.

11. **Klöckner Werke, Wettbewerb** manufacturing/
engineering, Germany
Stankowski + Duschek, Germany, 1950
A rotating motif suggests a smooth and precise mechanical action for a machine construction and plant engineering firm.

12. **One Housing Group** housing association, UK
Blast, UK, 2007
Symbol supporting the housing association's mission to 'work together to build sustainable communities'.

13. **Ready Rent All** transport, USA
Arnold Saks Associates, USA, 1968
A series of rotating rectangles suggests motion and transit in this symbol for a coast-to-coast rental franchise.

14. **Solargise** energy, UK and India
Mind Design, UK, 2009
This symbol for a company specializing in solar energy draws inspiration from the sun.

15. **The Australian Department of Trade and Industry** government, Australia
Steiner&Co., Hong Kong, 1966
A dynamic symbol based on the boomerang – an Australian icon familiar all over the world.

16. **Lake Parade** events, Switzerland
Areadesign, Switzerland, 2000
This symbol is part of an identity designed to promote a festival parade along the shores of Lake Geneva.

17. **Edizioni del Diaframma** publishing, Italy
Giancarlo Iliprandi, Italy, 1963
Symbol resembling an opening/closing aperture (*diaframma* in Italian).

18. **Cole Taylor Bank** finance, USA
Crosby Associates, USA, 2001
Distinctive symbol for a leading bank aiming to become the premier bank for Chicago area businesses and the people who own and manage them.

19.

20.

21.

22.

23.

24.

19. TCO consultancy/information technology, UK
A2 Design, UK, 2004
New mark for a software design consultancy,
aimed at reflecting the size and scope of a
growing business.

20. Albright-Knox Art Gallery arts and culture, USA
Chermayeff & Geismar, USA, 1965
A distinctly modern mark for an art gallery
in Buffalo.

21. Sitges Vila de Festivals tourism, Spain
Marnich Associates, Spain, 2008
A vibrant mark designed to promote tourism
in the Catalonian city of Sitges.

**22. International Islamic Trade Finance
Corporation** finance, Saudi Arabia
Siegel+Gale, USA, 2009
The client's mission is to advance trade and
improve the economic situation across the
Islamic world.

23. Norik sub sport and leisure, Slovenia
OS design studio, Slovenia, 2006
This symbol sets an aquatic tone for a diving
school and equipment store.

**24. MUNCYT, Museum of Science and Technology
of Spain** arts and culture, Spain
El Paso, Galería de Comunicación, Spain, 2008
This dynamic symbol is made up of question
marks, echoing science's ongoing quest for
answers.

25. Brooklyn Historical Society arts and culture, USA
Pentagram, USA, 2005
Institution dedicated to the appreciation of what
is arguably New York's most popular borough.

25.

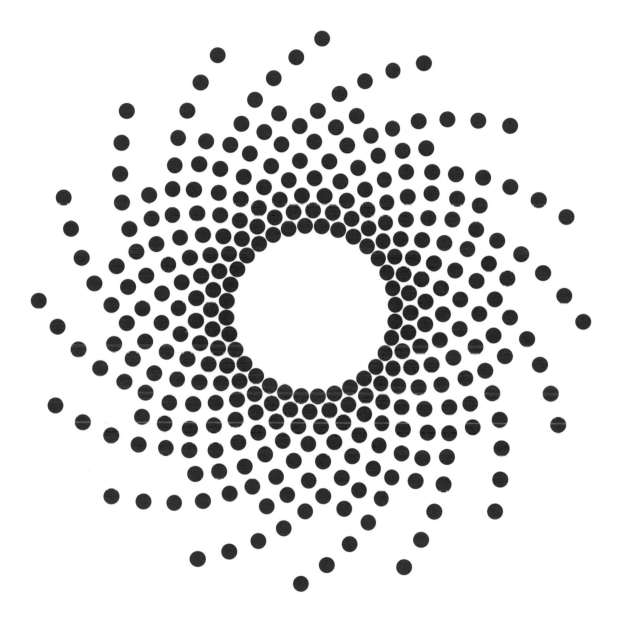

1.

2.

3.

4.

5.

1. **Proteus, Inc.** biomedical, USA
    Howard York/YorkBranding, USA, 1981
    Stylized algae represent the raw materials used
    by Proteus to develop a range of bio-industrial
    products.

2. **Laboratoires d'Etudes Cosmétologiques
    L.E.B.** health and beauty, France
    Jacques Nathan-Garamond, France, 1969
    Warm, approachable mark designed for
    a beauty product brand.

3. **CINOVA** design, Italy
    Waibl Heinz Studio Signo, Italy, 1984
    A chair-like motif suggests comfort, quality
    and contemporary design for this furniture
    design company.

4. **The Royal Academy of Engineering**
    education, UK
    Spencer du Bois, UK, 2004
    The first technology – the Neolithic hand-axe –
    is developed into an elegant symbol of the
    evolving relationship between people and
    technology.

5. **Al Qurashi** health and beauty, Saudi Arabia
    Coley Porter Bell, UK, 2008
    An organic symbol for a perfume specialist
    hints at the brand's Arabian heritage.

1.

2.

3.

4.

5.

6.

7.

8.

9.

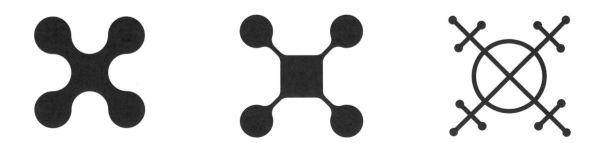

10.

11.

1. **FIVE Career Advisors** recruitment, USA
   Lodge Design, USA, 2008
   A stylized first-aid cross indicates the specialist area of this recruitment agency.
2. **Allens Arthur Robinson** legal, Australia
   Sadgrove Design, Australia, 2001
   Symbol for one of the largest law firms in the Asia–Pacific region.
3. **Advocate Healthcare** healthcare, USA
   Crosby Associates, USA, 1996
   Symbol representing a group of hospitals, clinics, graduate medical education and allied health programmes.
4. **Council of Catholic Men** religion, Canada
   William Newton and Jurgen Hoffman, Canada, 1968
   A stylized cross for a religious group in Toronto.

5. **Nelson** retail/technology, USA
   Unimark International, USA, c.1970s
   Mark designed for a division of the Nelson Sales Corporation.
6. **Interpoint** retail, USA
   Unimark International, USA, c.1973
   New name and identity for a company formerly known as the Food Facilities Management Corporation. Interpoint specializes in supplying food and beverages to interstate service stations.
7. **2SER 107.3** broadcasting, Australia
   Mark Gowing, Australia, 2002
   Modern mark reflecting the policies of a Sydney community radio station broadcasting a diverse and challenging range of music.

8. **Ancor** design, Italy
   Studio FM Milano, Italy, 2000
   A distinctly modern mark for a design company specializing in modular office furniture.
9. **Pecunia** fashion, Australia
   THERE, Australia, 2006
   A distinctive mark for a fashion brand. *Pecunia* is Latin for money or wealth.
10. **Savitra** energy, Spain
    Cruz más Cruz, Spain, 2007
    While *savitra* means solar, the symbol for this producer of clean energy also suggests other alternative energy sources, such as wind.
11. **Heathrow Express** transport, UK
    Glazer, UK, 2006
    A sophisticated mark suggesting the convenience and style that define the Heathrow Express service.

12.

13.

14.

15.

12. St John Ambulance healthcare, UK
Glazer, UK, 2007
Part of a broader project aimed at improving
recognition of the UK's leading first-aid charity,
the stylized cross draws on the St John
Ambulance heritage.

**13. XTVL (Xarxa de Televisions Locals de
Catalunya)** broadcasting, Spain
ruiz+company, Spain, 2008
A bold and distinctly modern symbol for a network
of local TV channels in the Catalan region.

14. Adamed healthcare, Poland
Karol Sliwka, Poland, 1990
A human figure combines with a 'medical
cross' in this symbol for a research and drug
development company.

15. Consejo Superior de Cámaras
government, Spain
Cruz más Cruz, Spain, 1998
A striking symbol expressing strength and unity,
designed for Spain's Superior Council of Trade
Chambers.

16. Raychem Corporation manufacturing, USA
*John Rieben/Raychem Corporation
Communications Department, USA, 1995*
Mark for a company specializing in self-regulating
heat-tracing technology.

17. TonenGeneral Sekiyu K.K. energy, Japan
Katsuichi Ito Design Office, Japan, 2000
A distinctive mark for one of Japan's leading
petroleum and petrochemical companies.

18. Atrius Health healthcare, USA
BrandEquity, USA, 2007
Two interlocking hearts reinforce the focus on
health of this non-profit physicians' organization.

19. Meromed Laboratories healthcare, Germany
Zinc, Argentina, 2007
A modern interpretation of a first-aid cross
supports a spirit of innovation and discovery.

16.

17.

18.

19.

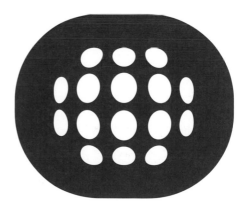

20.

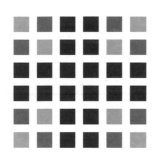

21.

22.

23.

24.

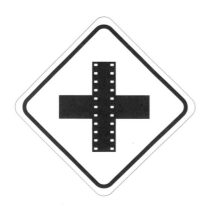

25.

26.

27.

28.

29.

20. Hellenic Republic restaurants, Australia
Anne Angel Designs, Australia, 2008
A mosaic symbol adopts the colours of the
Hellenic flag, evoking a sense of heritage and
pride for this Greek restaurant.

21. Restaurant Kaerajaan restaurants, Estonia
LOOVVOOL, Estonia, 2007
The name Kaerajaan comes from Estonian
folklore; the symbol adopts traditional patterns in
a contemporary way.

22. Riyadh International Airport transport,
Saudi Arabia
Howard York/YorkBranding, USA, 1978
Based on a triangular grid, this symbol for a
vast airport development suggests flight and
also mirrors the architectural master plan for
the airport's terminals.

23. Mikkeli Church religion, Finland
Kari Piippo, Finland, 1987
This symbol combines familiar Christian
iconography with the steep pitched roof common
to Finnish churches.

24. Crossroad Films film, USA
Pentagram, USA, 1989
An effective and literal translation of the client's
name, the symbol adopts the visual vocabulary
of road signs for this production company.

25. Katrina Coalition charity, USA
Hughes design/communications, USA, 2005
Crossed hands express strength through unity
in this symbol for a charity providing relief to
victims of Hurricane Katrina.

26. Tehran Graphic Design Syndicate professional
association, Iran
Ghobad Shiva, Iran, 1976
A cross composed of pencils communicates
the idea of unified strength for this syndicate
of graphic designers.

27. Heart Hospital of New Mexico healthcare, USA
Macnab Design, USA, 1998
This symbol uses a cross, a heart and a simple
colour change to introduce a helping-hand
element.

28. Rhode Island Department of Health
healthcare, USA
Malcolm Grear Designers, USA, 2007
Symbol emphasizing the department's focus
on people and suggesting that each person is
dependent upon the next one.

29. Presbyterian Church religion, USA
Malcolm Grear Designers, USA, 1985
Familiar religious iconography with a modern
twist features in this symbol for the American
Presbyterian Church, headquartered in Louisville,
Kentucky.

Swiss Federal Railway
(SBB CFF FFS)

Public transport, Switzerland
Various, Switzerland, 1972–78

A government institution until 1999, Switzerland's national rail company is now a special stock corporation, with all shares held by the Swiss Confederation or its cantons (member states). It sounds like a rather cooperative approach to corporate ownership, but having travelled on SBB CFF FFS trains, it does not seem to have compromised the comfort or efficiency of the network. Moreover, it is an approach that is reflected in the genesis of its identity, created between 1972 and 1978 by some of Switzerland's most celebrated designers.

Hans Hartmann laid the foundations in 1972 and Uli Huber played his part in 1976 before Josef Müller-Brockmann and Carlo Vivarelli applied the finishing touches in 1978. The inspiration for this timeless symbol, as for many Swiss institutions, is the Swiss flag – a beautifully balanced red square with a bold, equilateral white cross. The railway symbol adds an arrow to either end of the horizontal, suggesting notions of rail travel in much the same way as symbols designed for other national rail networks. However, the stroke of genius here is the extended, horizontal red ground: the cross/arrow motif sits in the right half while the left half remains red, a simple device that manages to express the motion of travel. It might have taken six years to find the right balance, but clearly it was time well spent.

The initials SBB CFF FFS communicate the railway's official name in the three core languages spoken in Switzerland: SBB stands for Schweizerische Bundesbahnen (German); CFF for Chemins de fer fédéraux Suisses (French); and FFS for Ferrovie Federali Svizzere (Italian).

1.

2.

3.

4.

5.

6.

7.

8.

9.

10.

1. **Edosa – Ediciones de Occidente S.A.**
   publishing, Spain
   Amand Domènech, Spain, 1964
   A publisher's imprint specializing in Western
   literature.

2. **Försäkringskassan** government, Sweden
   Dolhem Design, Sweden, 2002
   A modern reinterpretation of a symbol originally
   designed in 1970 for a social benefits organization.

3. **CDTI** technology, Spain
   Cruz más Cruz, Spain, 1980
   A 3-D arrow suggests progress in this symbol
   for the Centre for the Development of Industrial
   Technology.

4. **Weyerhaeuser** sustainable products, USA
   Lippincott, USA, 1958
   A simple, iconic symbol supports the company's
   aim to solve myriad problems by 'releasing the
   potential in trees' (still in use).

5. **Supra** chemicals, Sweden
   Olle Eksell, Sweden, 1968
   Symbol designed for a division of Superfos, a
   Swedish company supplying farmers with artificial
   fertlizer and other products.

6. **National Elevator Cab Company**
   manufacturing, USA
   Howard York/YorkBranding, USA, 1968
   A simple device hints at the end product made
   possible by a company specializing in fibreglass
   elevator cabs.

7. **Polo – Consultoria e Planejamento Ltda.**
   town planning, Brazil
   *João Carlos Cauduro and Ludovico Martino,
   Brazil, 1969*
   Symbol for a town-planning company based
   in São Paolo.

8. **EuroShop** tourism, Germany
   Uwe Loesch, Germany, 1978
   Arrows symbolize the selling process and the
   coming together of visitors at an international
   trade fair for retail business, which takes place
   every three years in Düsseldorf.

9. **Fabrika embalaze 29 novembre**
   manufacturing, Serbia
   Albert Kastelec, Serbia, 1959
   Converging arrows reflect the business of this
   packaging company.

10. **Ausa** transport, Argentina
    Cruz más Cruz, Spain, 1974
    Two arrows provide Ausa Autopistas Argentinas
    (Argentinian Motorways) with a dynamic symbol.

11.

12.

13.

14.

15.

16.

11. **Intranszmas** transport, Hungary
Nándor Gremsperger, Hungary, 1967
Two arrows suggest outbound and return
journeys.

12. **NY State Urban Development Corp** urban
development, USA
Arnold Saks Associates, USA, 1980
Symbol suggesting the client's positive and
focused mission to improve inner-city areas.

13. **Amtrak** transport, USA
Lippincott, USA, 1971
Iconic symbol for the USA's National Railroad
Passenger Corporation; the mark has since been
modernized.

14. **Stimmabgabe** media/technology, Germany
Nalindesign, Germany, 2004
Themes of equalization support an audio-
production company specializing in
synchronization.

15. **Snap** Internet/retail, Switzerland
Areadesign, Switzerland, 2002
Symbol for a top-up-card alternative to credit
and debit cards, designed specifically for Internet
shopping.

16. **Facility for Advancing Water Biofiltration
(FAWB)** research/technology, Australia
Inkahoots, Australia, 2006
A research facility at Monash University,
Melbourne exploring new technologies for
urban water management.

17. **Nederlandse Spoorwegen** transport,
The Netherlands
Teldesign, The Netherlands, 1968
An iconic symbol for the Dutch rail network.
The arrows represent the outgoing and return
journeys and the two lines in the middle represent
the track.

18. **CityRail** transport, Australia
Cato Partners, Australia, 1999
This revitalized symbol for one of the world's
largest commuter networks energized the
established identity while capturing the speed
and motion of rail travel.

17.

18.

British Rail

Public transport, UK
Design Research Unit, UK, 1965

British Rail emerged in 1965 from the ashes of British Railways, the nationalized rail network created by Clement Atlee's Labour government in 1948. Prompted by a desire to shed the network's 'dowdy, steam-age' image – a response to the 1960s Beeching Report – the change of name was supported by a far more radical overhaul of the network's visual identity. At the time, it must have felt like a quantum leap. The new blue and white train liveries exuded a wholly contemporary air that was surpassed only by a new and brilliant symbol created by Design Research Unit.

Founded by Misha Black in 1943, DRU was a progressive studio driven by a desire to use design as a force for social good. The symbol for British Rail was drawn by Gerald Burney and represents two rail tracks heading in opposite directions, crossed by stylized 'points' that form arrows. Set on a dynamic red ground, it proved so effective that it quickly came to symbolize mainline rail travel in general and went on to influence the design of rail-network identities in other countries. Furthermore, it has stood the test of time: despite the privatization of the UK's rail network, DRU's symbol is still used by trains operated under the aegis of Network Rail.

Almost half a century since it was designed, it still looks fresh, standing head and shoulders above the frequently weak and ephemeral identities designed for the UK's myriad regional operators.

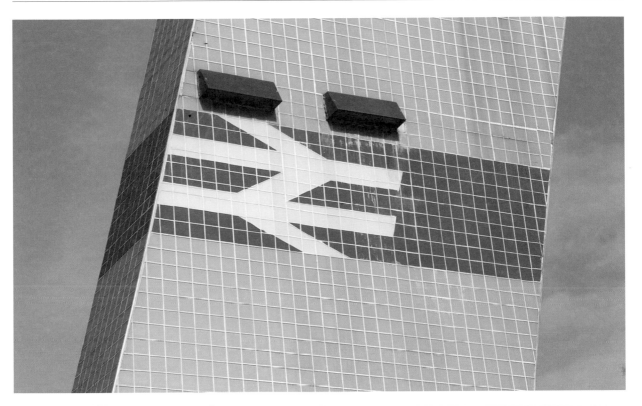

Look what you gain when you travel by train

Now: London to Bath, a comfortable 69 minutes

Now: London to Bristol Temple Meads, a smooth 85 minutes

Now: London to Cardiff, a relaxing 105 minutes

Now: London to Swansea, an easy 163 minutes

Pick up a free copy of the pocket timetable

Inter-City 125 makes the going easy

19.

20.

21.

22.

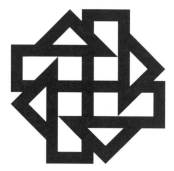

23.

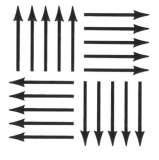

24.

25.

19. **PTM-Yhtiö Oy LKV** property, Finland
    Hahmo, Finland, 2005
    Two arrows converge to reveal a plot of land in
    this symbol for a company that buys and sells land
    for its clients.

20. **Recognition Devices** technology, USA
    Howard York/YorkBranding, USA, 1983
    Symbol for a company producing devices (such
    as pagers) used to locate individuals within
    a facility – a doctor in a hospital, for example.

21. **Corry Jamestown Corporation**
    manufacturing, USA
    Unimark International, USA, c.1970s
    Symbol for a manufacturer of office equipment
    and furnishings.

22. **Cuenca** events, Spain
    Cruz más Cruz, Spain, 1987
    A collection of arrows suggests the hillside
    architecture of the town of Cuenca. The symbol
    was designed for a cultural event.

23. **CIBA Scientific Information Service**
    research, USA
    Chermayeff & Geismar, USA, 1959
    A lively arrow formation suggests exploration
    in this symbol for a company producing scientific
    publications and research.

24. **Telecom Business Direction** telecoms,
    New Zealand
    Cato Partners, Australia, 1998
    This symbol for a chain of retail outlets wraps
    arrows round a sphere to suggest global
    communications.

25. **World Central Dubai** transport, UAE
    Cato Partners, Australia, 2006
    Traditional Arabic motifs embracing a globe
    reinforce the message that the world has a
    new central hub.

1.

2.

3.

4.

5.

6.

7.

8.

9.

1. **Austrian National Library** libraries, Austria
   Bohatsch Visual Communication GmbH,
   Austria, 2001
   A solid shape implies an open book and more
   for the Austrian state library.
2. **Comma Consulting** communications/
   consultancy, UK
   HGV Pierre Vermeir, UK, 2008
   A warm, approachable mark for a company
   that advises organizations on their internal
   communications.
3. **Centre de Chant Choral** music, Belgium
   Coast, Belgium, 2004
   A simple speech bubble/single quotation mark
   implies the vocal nature of this choral singing
   association.

4. **Talk** public relations, USA
   Morvil Advertising + Design Group, USA, 2005
   Single quotation marks set close together create
   a playful face, conveying the public relations
   theme with wit.
5. **Encore Careers** non-profit organizations, USA
   Landor Associates, international, 2009
   A semicolon suggests the career pause
   experienced by baby boomers. This symbol is for
   an initiative helping people to start new, second
   careers in rewarding areas such as healthcare,
   sustainability and education.
6. **Dunya TV** broadcasting, Pakistan
   Cato Partners, Australia, 2007
   A new tagline, 'Voice and Vision', inspired the
   symbol for a new television network in Pakistan.

7. **dbase (RDD Design Network)** design, Austria
   Q2 Design, Austria, 2001
   An elongated speech bubble suggests dialogue.
8. **Superstore Inc.** arts and culture, Japan
   Good Design Company, Japan, 2004
   Symbol for an artist-management agency.
9. **Bolinda Audio** publishing, Australia
   Hoyne Design, Australia, 2004
   An open book in a speech bubble sums up the
   business of one of Australia's leading audio-book
   publishers.

10.

11.

12.

13.

14.

15.

16.

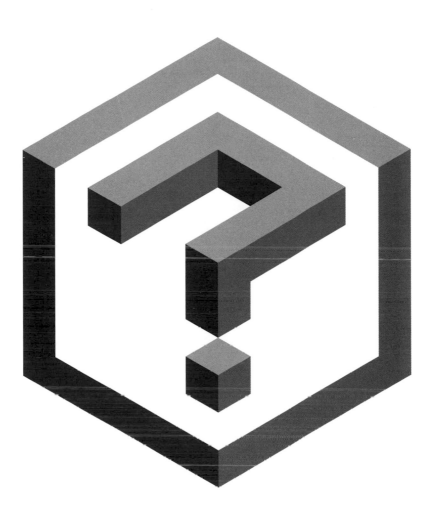

10. DIA retail, Spain
Interbrand, international, 2006
This mark revitalizes the existing percentage
symbol and is part of a broader identity refresh
for Carrefour's Spanish discount grocery chain.

11. Newsgrade Internet, USA
Pentagram, USA, 2000
Internet service offering financial news and
real-time financial data on publicly traded
companies worldwide.

12. Youmeus Design design, UK
Accept & Proceed, UK, 2003
The mark for this product company presents
a visual interpretation of the client's name.

13. Nonsuch Films film, USA
Pentagram, USA, 1990
A bold symbol suggests Nonsuch Films has
no equal in its field.

14. Motorola Digital DNA telecoms, USA
Pentagram, USA, 1998
The symbol for Motorola's 'embedded solutions'
division expresses technical integrity with a
friendly, organic tone.

15. Arts Council Lottery Funding
arts and culture, UK
Pentagram, UK, 1997
A mark designed to identify Arts Council projects
benefiting from National Lottery funding.

16. Futuretrack education/charity, UK
Funnel Creative, UK, 2007
Simple graphic device responding to
Futuretrack's survey into how and why
students make career decisions.

REPRESENTATIONAL

1.

2.

3.

4.

5.

6.

7.

8.

9.

10.

11.

12.

13.

1. **Watermark Mortgage Group** finance, USA
    Morvil Advertising + Design Group, USA, 2008
    A distinctive interpretation of the client's name
    avoids visual clichés to create a refreshing,
    modern look.
2. **Instituto Cubano del Petróleo** energy, Cuba
    Félix Beltrán, Cuba, 1968
    Symbol for a campaign to conserve petrol.
3. **Econia** food and beverages, Ukraine
    Headshot brand development, Ukraine, 2007
    Three drops symbolize the brand's environmental
    values and the purity of the water they sell.
4. **Monroe County Pure Waters Agency**
    infrastructure, USA
    R. Roger Remington, USA, 1976
    This symbol communicates the organization's
    aim to reduce pollution in Irondequoit Bay,
    the Genesee River, areas of Lake Ontario and
    other Monroe County waters.

5. **Palm Beach Couture** fashion, USA
    Layfield Design, Australia, 2005
    Waves and leaves combine to provide a
    beachwear fashion label with an elegant,
    aspirational mark.
6. **River East Arts Center** arts and education, USA
    Essex Two, USA, 1995
    A sense of place and a progressive spirit define
    this symbol for a community-focused arts-related
    development.
7. **Clearwater, Inc.** public utilities, USA
    Wink, Incorporated, USA, 2000
    Identity for a water treatment company that
    replenishes and restores the quality of water
    in public lakes.
8. **Triton** exploration, UK
    Funnel Creative, UK, 2008
    A hand-drawn symbol provides a suitably nautical
    theme for an underwater exploration company.
9. **Cape Fear Public Utilities Authority**
    public utilities, USA
    Morvil Advertising + Design Group, USA, 2008
    A clean, modern look for a utilities brand; the
    water refers to Cape Fear's riverside location.

10. **South East Water** public utilities, Australia
    Cato Partners, Australia, 1995
    Ripples of water convey both the basic nature
    of the service and that the company is
    forward-thinking.
11. **Desert Water Company** public utilities, USA
    Denis Parkhurst, USA, 2000
    Symbol for a water company supplying Palm
    Springs, California.
12. **Madero Walk** property development, Argentina
    Fileni & Fileni Design, Argentina, 2008
    This symbol for a development positioned as
    'Latin America's first floating cultural center'
    adopts ever-decreasing circles. Commissioned
    by property developers Vizora.
13. **ICES CIEM** exploration, Denmark
    Punktum Design, Denmark, 2007
    Evocative mark for the world's oldest
    intergovernmental organization for marine and
    fisheries science.

1.

2.

3.

4.

1. **Sneje** jeweller, Russia
   Ony, Russia, 2007
   Symbol for a collection of jewellery designed, like snowflakes, to be unique.
2. **FusionOne** technology, USA
   Method Inc., USA, 2000
   This modern mark for a pioneering technology brand evokes points connected through a central node.

3. **Arlberg Marketing GmbH** tourism, Austria
   Bohatsch Visual Communication GmbH, Austria, 2006
   An elaborate snowflake hints at the wintry landscapes of Austria's Arlberg mountain range.
4. **Snowy Hydro** energy, New Zealand
   Cato Partners, Australia, 1990
   Mark symbolizing snow being melted by the sun to produce the essential element for hydroelectric power.

5. **Hokusetu** paper, Japan
   Ken Miki & Associates, Japan, 1996
   Hokusetu translates as 'snow mountain'; the name and symbol reflect the Heiwa Paper Co. Ltd's successful attempt to develop a paper 'as white as snow'.
6. **Aeroprof** air conditioning/engineering, Russia
   RockBee Design, Russia, 2008
   A simple snowflake, but a closer look at the eight components reveals images that correspond to each of the company's eight service areas.

5.

6.

1.

1. **Brandschutz Keuchel** emergency services, Germany
   Lockstoff Design, Germany, 2009
   This soft blue flame seems well under control –
   ideal for an agency dealing in fire protection.
2. **Kinetik Energy** Energy, Australia
   Cato Partners, Australia, 1997
   Communicating a sense of dynamic energy
   through the use of multiple images of a gas flame.
3. **Stavby Barvy Morava** property, Germany
   Toman Graphic Design, Czech Republic, 2003
   The symbol recalls the client's origins as a paint
   supplies shop before it expanded to offer
   construction services.
4. **38** energy, UK
   Sam Dallyn, UK, 2003
   A simple mark reflecting the nature of the
   business in a bold, contemporary manner.

5. **HarperCollins** publishing, UK
   Chermayeff & Geismar, USA, 1990
   When Harper & Row, with its torch logo, merged
   with William Collins, with its fountain symbol, an
   opportunity was born. The symbol combines fire
   and water, hinting at the brand's heritage while
   creating a distinctive mark for a new company.
6. **First Source** purchasing agency, UK
   Thomas Manss & Company, Germany, 2000
   A pictorial symbol made from the reconstructed
   elements of the letter 's' expresses a seamless
   service connecting suppliers and customers.
7. **Gaslink** energy, Ireland
   Creative Inc., Ireland, 2006
   A stylized flame symbolizes the independent
   system operator responsible for developing
   and maintaining Ireland's natural gas
   transportation system.
8. **Alvheim** energy, USA
   Rune Mortensen, Norway, 2005
   Symbol for the Alvheim North Sea oil field,
   commissioned by the project leader Marathon
   Oil Corporation.

9. **Silke Weggen** hairdressing, Germany
   Nalindesign, Germany, 2008
   Flowing locks of hair symbolize a mobile
   hairdressing brand.
10. **Scribner** publishing, USA
    Pentagram, USA, 1995
    A revitalized version of Scribner's torch
    represents the notion that books provide
    illumination.
11. **New York University** education, USA
    Chermayeff & Geismar, USA, 1972
    This stylized torch, a New York icon, has identified
    the university's ever-expanding facilities for nearly
    40 years.
12. **Nakheel** property development, UAE
    Dragon Rouge, international, 2007
    This symbol is part of a revitalized identity for
    a property developer responsible for creating
    landmark destinations in Dubai such as the Palm
    Trilogy, the World and the Waterfront.
13. **KAZE no ENNICHI designale '93** events, Japan
    Ken Miki & Associates, Japan, 1993
    A lively flame symbol commissioned by the
    Designale Osaka Committee for this Japanese
    design event.

2.

3.

4.

5.

6.

7.

8.

9.

10.

11.

12.

13.

1.

2.

3.

4.

5.

6.

7.

8.

9.

10.

11.

1. **Agens** consultancy/employment,
   The Netherlands
   Total Identity Amsterdam bv, The Netherlands, 2009
   The figure's positive strength supports the
   personality of a company providing employee
   reintegration services.
2. **Linea Verde** retail, Italy
   Brunazzi&Associati, Italy, 1991
   A simplified floral mark for a garden centre.
3. **Just Cotton** manufacturing, UK
   10 Associates, UK, 2007
   A range of 100% pure cotton bedding from
   the UK's leading manufacturer of pillows
   and duvets.
4. **Parque Arauco** construction/property
   development, Argentina
   Fileni & Fileni Design, Argentina, 2005
   A simplified floral mark for a Santiago-based
   company specializing in the development of
   shopping malls.

5. **Pension HERZ** finance, Japan
   Katsuichi Ito Design Office, Japan, 1997
   Abstract imagery suggesting nature helps to
   create a warm, approachable brand personality.
6. **Si J'étais Moi** health and beauty, Switzerland
   Vingtneuf degres sàrl, Switzerland, 2008
   Elegant floral motif for a day spa.
7. **Akashi Kaikyo National Government
   Park** tourism, Japan.
   Ken Miki & Associates, Japan, 2002
   A stylized flower evokes the natural beauty of
   a national park on Awaji Island in Japan's Seto
   Inland Sea.
8. **Australian Conservation
   Foundation** government, Australia
   *David Lancashire Design with Ken Cato,
   Australia, 2004*
   A metamorphosis of the ACF's previous symbol,
   this one has a subtle illustrative element that
   suggests an organic tone.

9. **Wiener Städtische** insurance, Austria
   Alessandri Design, Austria, 2004
   A flourishing business, Wiener Städtische is the
   leading Austrian insurance group in central and
   eastern Europe.
10. **Visionary Living** interior design, UK
    Aboud Creative, UK, c.2000s
    Simplicity and elegance define this mark for
    an interiors and artificial flower company.
11. **Prolet Clothing** clothing and
    accessories, Bulgaria
    Stefan Kanchev, Bulgaria, c.1960s–70s
    An overtly modern floral device reflects
    the name and 'proletarian' aesthetic of this
    particular clothing brand.

12.

13.

14.

15.

16.

17.

12. Dermadental healthcare, Ireland
Area, Ireland, 2009
A soft, aspirational symbol for Ireland's first combined facial aesthetic and dental spa.

13. Cruise 2 transport/travel, Ireland
Area, Ireland, 2009
A simple floral motif hints at the exotic climes visited by this cruise operator.

14. Joey's Yoga sport and leisure, Germany
SWSP Design, Germany, 2009
An illustrative floral motif suggests peace, tranquility and well-being – an ideal symbol for a yoga course.

15. Confetti retail, UK
Coley Porter Bell, UK, 2001
An elegant, celebratory image for a wedding-expert retailer with high-street and online presence.

16. Infacol pharmaceuticals, UK
Dew Gibbons, UK, 2007
A warm, natural symbol for a colic-relief product for babies, produced and marketed in the UK by Forest Laboratories.

17. Shinsegae Department Stores retail, South Korea
Chermayeff & Geismar, USA, 1999
Floral motif developed for a leading South Korean department-store chain.

18.

19.

20.

21.

22.

23.

18. HANAO Country Club sport and leisure, Japan
Katsuichi Ito Design Office, Japan, 1992
A painterly floral motif conveys the natural beauty
of this golf club's surrounding landscape.

19. ValleyCrest landscape design, USA
Attik, UK/USA, 2007
A stylized floral mark reflects the nature of the
business while striking a balance between organic
and sophisticated.

20. Takeda Engei chemicals, Japan
Katsuichi Ito Design Office, Japan, 1989
A hybrid floral motif suggests science and nature
for a brand of chemical gardening products.

21. Oglethorpe University education, USA
Pentagram, USA, 2007
The symbol for a liberal arts college in Atlanta,
Georgia, is based on a quatrefoil (an architectural
floral motif with four petals) at the entrance to the
college's Hermance Stadium.

22. Rosières manufacturing, France
Rudi Meyer/RSCG Paris, France, 1978
A rose/hob for a manufacturer of kitchen
appliances based in the French village of Rosières.

23. WATSU healthcare, Sweden
Riografik.ch, Switzerland, 2007
Watsu is an abbreviated term for water shiatsu,
the massage therapy suggested by this suitably
aquatic symbol.

24.

25.

26.

27.

28.

29.

24. Det Norske Arbeiderparti politics, Norway
Rune Mortensen, Norway, 2004
A modern interpretation of a familiar labour
movement icon, designed for the Norwegian
Labour Party.

25. Grandiflorum Perfumes health and beauty, USA
Elixir Design, USA, 1997
A luxurious mark for a perfume brand specializing
in the revival of historical techniques.

26. Social Democrats politics, Denmark
e-Types, Denmark, 2002
A stylized rose recalls the familiar symbolism
of left-wing politics.

27. Württembergische Bibelanstalt religion,
Germany
Stankowski + Duschek, Germany, c.1960s
This symbol for a religious institute employs the
same form, reduced in size and rotated five times,
to create layers of petals.

28. Hyperion publishing, USA
Louise Fili, USA, 1989
Symbol for a publishing division of Disney named
after the original studio's location on Hyperion
Avenue, Hollywood. An hyperion is a species of
day lily.

29. The Nishi-Nippon City Bank Ltd. finance, Japan
Bravis International Limited, Japan, 2004
The flower represents the bank's desire to grow
with its customers and help local businesses
to flourish.

30.

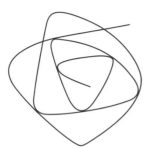

31.

32.

33.

30. Stoelzle Architekten architecture, Germany
*Büro Uebele Visuelle Kommunikation,
Germany, 1996*
This symbol for an architectural practice is a
visual representation of the process; projects
start at a predefined point and evolve in an almost
circular fashion.

31. Blue Ginger Spa sport and leisure, USA
Morvil Advertising + Design Group, USA, 2005
A languid, feminine mark suggesting tranquility
and natural treatments.

32. Mayflower Inn and Spa hospitality, USA
The O Group, USA, 2006
An elegant floral symbol captures the rural
serenity of this widely acclaimed luxury hotel
in Connecticut.

33. Just Be Well healthcare, UK
Attitude Design, UK, 2009
A floral motif provides an appropriate symbol
for a Harley Street practice specializing in
hypnotherapy.

34. Maui Bus transport, USA
Method Inc., USA, 2005
A functional, iconic symbol recalls local flora,
the notion of a compass rose and the concept
of navigation.

35. Consejo Federal de Turismo (CFT)
tourism, Argentina
Estudio Soma, Argentina, 2009
A floral motif suggests the natural beauty
of the Argentinian landscape.

36. BASE-MK property development, Kazakhstan
Pentagram, USA, 2007
A mark for a developer of luxurious residential,
retail and commercial properties in Asia, the
Middle East and Europe.

37. Six Sites for Sound events, UK
Mind Design, UK, 2007
Symbol for a Resonance FM exhibition on 'sound
art' in six different galleries and with one speaker
for each location.

38. Magnolia health and beauty, France
IP-3, France, 2002
A crafted magnolia made up of small dots conveys
a feminine yet undeniably modern tone.

39. Golden Star Tea Co. food and beverages, USA
Elixir Design, USA, 2008
A refined mark suggests the premium quality
and ingredients in Golden Star's innovative
sparkling floral tea.

34.

35.

36.

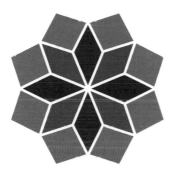

37.

38.

39.

RACE
(Research for an Alternative and Clean Energy)

Alternative energy, Italy
Metaforma Design, Italy, 2008

Established in 1981, RACE operates on an international stage with a range of innovative projects and activities fuelled by achievements obtained 'through a constant scientific research in the ecological and environmental fields: recycling strategic resources; environment safeguard and tutelage; recycling waste materials to produce clean energy'. Prompted by a desire to improve its international profile – and pre-empting the worldwide promotion and implementation of its innovative energy technologies – RACE invited Milan studio Metaforma Design to revitalize its identity.

Fêted as the Best of Italy at the 2008 WOLDAs (the Worldwide Logo Design Annual Awards), Metaforma's solution expresses both a respect for the environment and the need for energy. The leaf motif immediately suggests nature, while the gradual change of colour from green (nature) to orange (energy) echoes the non-invasive character of the technologies developed by RACE. The smooth and precise rotation of the leaf around an axis of 18 degrees reflects the fact that these technologies are grounded in scientific research and mathematical accuracy.

Attractive and versatile, the symbol is applied in a number of different colourways for each of RACE's constituent areas: chemistry, cosmetics, pharmaceuticals, waste disposal and food.

| INNOVATION AND RESEARCH | ENVIRONMENT AND WASTE | CLEAN ENERGY | ENVIRONMENT AND INDUSTRY |

| ENVIRONMENT AND INDUSTRY | ENVIRONMENT AND CHEMISTRY | PHARMACEUTICAL CHEMISTRY | FOOD CHEMISTRY |

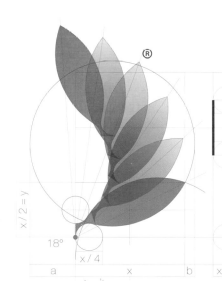

RACE

RESEARCH FOR AN ALTERNATIVE AND CLEAN ENERGY

Since 1981

1.

2.

3.

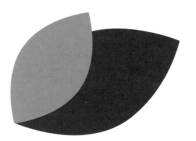

4.

5.

6.

7.

8.

9.

10.

1. **Agropure** food and beverages, USA
    Rule29 Creative, Inc., USA, date unknown
    A leaf motif suggests well-being in this symbol
    for a food brand whose products provide health
    and medical benefits.
2. **Crocus.co.uk** gardening, UK
    Pentagram, UK, 2000
    A fresh mark for an online gardening
    advice service.
3. **Mick Berry** landscape design, UK
    Delicious Industries, UK, 2006
    A simple graphic device that instantly
    communicates the nature of the business.
4. **CSR360 Global Partner Network** charity, UK
    Funnel Creative, UK, 2008
    Symbol based on a sinusoidal or map
    projection and designed in partnership with
    Erskine for Business in the Community, a Prince
    of Wales charity.
5. **Organic Stats** Internet, USA
    CMPLT Design, Germany, 2009
    A leaf motif suggests the organic growth
    fostered by this web-optimization and
    analytic service.
6. **Kwiaciarnia** retail, Poland
    Karol Sliwka, Poland, 1991
    A delicate yet bold and modern symbol for
    a florist.
7. **Plum'Art** retail, Switzerland
    Areadesign, Switzerland, 2000
    An elegant, contemporary mark for a furniture
    shop reflects its 'design and nature' theme.
8. **VierstroomZorgring** healthcare,
    The Netherlands
    Teldesign, The Netherlands, 2007
    A light, playful symbol for a home care
    organization operating throughout the west
    of The Netherlands.
9. **Greenbelt Group** property, UK
    Graven Images, UK, 2006
    This symbol is part of a customer-focused brand
    identity for the only UK-wide company that owns
    and manages greenbelt land formed as part of
    new housing developments.
10. **Istituto Ramazzini** medical research, Italy
    Waibl Heinz Studio Signo, Italy, 1987
    A symmetrical, organic mark conveys a suitably
    scientific tone for an oncological research institute.

11.

12.

13.

14.

15.

16.

17.

18.

19.

20.

21.

22.

23.

11. **Qatre** publishing, Iran
   Ebrahim Haghighi, Iran, 1985
   The symbol for a publisher combines an open
   book with a drop shape (*qatre* in Persian).
12. **Sarv** publishing, Iran
   Ebrahim Haghighi, Iran, 1981
   A bold, confident cypress leaf (*sarv* is Persian
   for cypress).
13. **GardenJot** Internet, USA
   Siah Design, USA, 2009
   A pen/leaf device for an online network aimed
   at connecting local gardeners.
14. **Rochester Institute of Technology**
   International Garden public space, USA
   R. Roger Remington, USA, 1969
   A modern leaf motif for a public garden in
   an historic higher-education institute in New
   York State.
15. **AZRRI** government, Croatia
   Parabureau, Croatia, 2005
   A leaf device reflects the mission of a rural
   development agency focused on the Istrian
   peninsula.

16. **OEC (Ohio Environmental Council)**
   environmental advocacy, USA
   9MYLES, Inc., USA, 2009
   An elegant mark for an organization working
   to ensure healthy air, land and water for
   Ohio residents.
17. **FROM** government, Spain
   Cruz más Cruz, Spain, 2001
   Three fish combine to create a plantlike form in
   this symbol for Spain's Ministry of Agriculture
   and Fishing.
18. **TEE CRM Software** technology, USA
   Siah Design, USA, 2008
   A warm approachable symbol designed for
   a brand providing customer relationship
   management software.
19. **IDP** education, Australia
   Cato Partners, Australia, 2001
   A 'tree of knowledge' spreads over the globe
   to promote worldwide registration at Australia's
   universities.

20. **Centrum Stomatologiczne**
   Eurodental healthcare, Poland
   Karol Sliwka, Poland, 1990
   Symbol for a dental practice.
21. **Verein Oberlinhaus** social welfare, Germany
   Studio Regular/wegewerk GmbH, Germany, 2005
   A restructuring process divided this historic
   welfare organization into four areas, unified again
   in this symbol.
22. **Hilliard Food** restaurants, UK
   Spin, UK, 2005
   Four petals suggest the seasonal produce on
   sale at a 'gastro café' near St Paul's Cathedral
   in London.
23. **International Agriplex** agriculture, USA
   Howard York/YorkBranding, USA, 1982
   This symbol is part of an identity for a centre in
   Florida where delegates from around the world
   gathered to discuss agricultural issues.

24.

25.

26.

27.

28.

29.

30.

24. Nørrebro Bryghus food and beverages, Denmark
Punktum Design, Denmark, 2003
This is part of a family of symbols, each of which
varies in colour to suggest the ingredients employed
to create Denmark's first carbon-neutral beer.

25. Land Heritage agriculture/charity, UK
Together Design Ltd, UK, 2004
Designed for a charitable trust committed to the
protection and promotion of organic farming in
the UK, this symbol illustrates the charity's love
of the land.

26. Palm Jumeirah tourism, UAE
Dragon Rouge, international, 2008
Symbol conveying the elegant luxury of a Dubai
development resplendent with hotels, residential
property, shopping and leisure attractions.

27. Tertti Manor hospitality, Finland
Kari Piippo, Finland, 2002
Natural mark suggesting the location of a
manor-house hotel and restaurant in the heart
of lakeland Finland.

28. Landscapes Unique landscape design, USA
Morvil Advertising + Design Group, USA, 2008
A simplified leaf form is overlapped several times
to create an ethereal and harmonious symbol.

29. Muehlenbusch Apotheke healthcare, Germany
Lockstoff Design, Germany, 2007
A soft, natural mark for a high street pharmacy
in Dormagen.

**30. The Woodlands Resort & Conference
Center** hospitality, USA
Pinkerton Design, USA, 2002
Evocative symbol for a forest retreat only 30
minutes from downtown Houston, Texas.

31.

32.

33.

34.

35.

36.

37.

31. Margaret Josefin Japan Co., Ltd. health and
beauty, Japan
Ken Miki & Associates, Japan, 1995
An elegant, feminine mark for one of Japan's
leading cosmetics brands.

32. Castles, Wood and Water public space, UK
Funnel Creative, UK, 2006
A common woodland fern depicts the
regeneration of woodlands and water. It was
designed in partnership with Erskine for Castle
Morpeth Borough Council.

33. Miljøpartiet De Grønne politics, Norway
Rune Mortensen, Norway, 2006
Symbol supporting the environmental agenda
of Norway's Green Party.

34. Cherry Garden Clinic healthcare, Russia
Superred, Russia, 2008
An elegant cherry-blossom motif suggests
well-being while communicating the clinic's name.

35. The Good Grain Company food and
beverages, UK
Dragon Rouge, international, 2008
A wholesome mark reflects the brand's refusal
to add unnecessary ingredients to its products.

36. Brooklyn Botanic Garden arts and culture, USA
Carbone Smolan Agency, USA, 2004
Elegant and vibrant, this stylized plant symbol
supports the garden's strapline: 'Where plants
come to life'.

37. Carbis Bay Hotel hospitality, UK
Absolute Design, UK, 2005
A wistful symbol for a hotel in Cornwall suggests
both a sense of place and a feeling of tranquillity.

1.

2.

3.

4.

5.

6.

1. **MorseLife** property, USA
   BrandEquity, USA, 2006
   Symbol integrating the 'tree of life' with the Star of David to reinforce the cultural heritage of these Jewish retirement homes.
2. **Hokkaido Takushoku Bank** finance, Japan
   Shigeo Fukuda, Japan, 1969
   Symbol evoking nature for a leading bank on Japan's northern island of Hokkaido.

3. **Finsilva** forest administration, Finland
   Porkka & Kuutsa, Finland, 2005
   An evocative fir cone/tree symbol designed for a company focused on the ownership and economic management of Finland's forests.
4. **Canadian Pulp & Paper** professional associations, Canada
   Kissiloff & Wimmershoff Inc., Canada, 1967
   Two simplified trees reflect the industry's raw materials, and imply the partnerships formed between companies.

5. **Strategico** finance, Australia.
   Naughtyfish design, Australia, 2007
   The symbol for a financial planning firm supports the brand values of growth, wealth and protection.
6. **AEK Bank 1826** finance, Switzerland
   Nordland, Switzerland, 2006
   Trees with their branches pointing upwards establish a positive spirit for a Swiss cooperative bank.

7.

8.

9.

10.

11.

12.

7. **Jerusalem Botanical Gardens** arts and
    culture, Israel
    Dan Reisinger, Israel, 1987
    A simple tree motif is invested with characteristics
    of Hebrew calligraphy.
8. **Jay Peak** tourism, USA
    Ken Parkhurst and Jayme Rodgers, USA, 1974
    Symbol for a community and ski resort in Vermont,
    just 11 km (7 miles) south of the Canadian border.

9. **Føroya Sparikassi** finance, Faroe Islands
    Punktum Design, Denmark, 2003
    Symbol suggesting growth for the largest and
    oldest bank in the Faroe Islands.
10. **Trinity Dental** healthcare, USA
    Lodge Design, USA, 2008
    This symbol blends traditional and modern
    aesthetics to reflect the strength and growth
    of the business.

11. **Shadow Wood** property development, USA
    The Brothers Bogusky, USA, 1989
    An evocative mark echoes the name of a
    condominium development in Miami.
12. **East Coast Greenway** public space, USA
    Pentagram, USA, 2003
    A pastoral mark – complete with reflection – for a
    4830 km (3000 mile) traffic-free path linking cities
    from Maine to Florida.

13.

14.

15.

16.

17.

18.

19.

20.

21.

22.

13. Linnaeus University education, Sweden
Stockholm Design Lab, Sweden, 2009
This 'tree of knowledge' was inspired by a sketch
made by the university's namesake, the Swedish
botanist Carl Linnaeus.

14. Mulberry fashion, UK
FOUR IV, UK, 2001–02
A modern reinterpretation of an existing mulberry-
tree logo for a luxury English fashion brand.

15. The Natural Family Day events/healthcare, UK
Delicious Industries, UK, 2005
A rustic symbol for a family-orientated health fair
is simple and bold enough to be applied as a
rubber stamp.

16. Lemanski Gartenbau landscape design, Poland
Logotypy.com, Poland, 2007
An elegant tree motif provides a clear indication of
the client's area of specialism in landscape design.

17. Capella construction, UK
Fivefootsix, UK, 2008
An oak tree designed for a manufacturer of
bespoke wood shutters evokes a sense of
classic English quality whilst providing shade
and protection.

18. Campos de Oriente agriculture, Argentina
and Uruguay
Design Has No Name (DHNN), Argentina, 2008
A tree in full bloom suggests the focus of an
organization supporting farming concerns.

19. Greenwoods clothing and accessories, UK
Studio Ten and a Half, UK, 2009
A revitalized symbol for one of the UK's leading
high street suit-hire and clothing chains.

20. Portsea Estate food and beverages, Australia
Naughtyfish design, Australia, 2004
An evocative tree expresses the natural
terrain of a vineyard on southern Australia's
Mornington Peninsula.

21. Editions de l'Olivier publishing, France
Pentagram, UK, 1991
This symbol is a graphic play on the owner's
first name, Olivier, which is French for olive tree.

22. The Gardens Shop arts and culture, Australia
David Lancashire Design, Australia, 2004
A cornucopia of leaves and fruit for a souvenir
shop at the entrance to the Royal Botanic
Gardens, Melbourne.

1.

2.

1. **Teachernet** education, UK
HSAG, UK, 2002
An 'apple for the teacher' represents an online education resource set up by the Department for Education and Skills.

2. **Vegetable Bar** food and beverages, Germany
Magpie Studio, UK, 2007
Witty mark for an impromptu venue that springs up each evening after the vegetable market has closed.

3. **Fresh Fruit Baskets** retail, USA
Siah Design, USA, 2009
Fruit segments are transformed into a basket in this symbol for an online fruit basket delivery service.

4. **Piperlime** fashion/retail, USA
Pentagram, USA, 2006
The symbol for a Gap-owned online footwear and accessories retailer plays on the name's fruitier qualities.

5. **Hotel Traube Tonbach** hospitality, Germany
Claus Koch, Germany, 1998
This symbol for a hotel with a reputation for exceptional dining combines both the traditonal and the modern.

6. **Pumpkin Pet Products** retail, UK
Dowling Design & Art Direction, UK, 2008
A witty visual take on the unusual name for a retail outlet selling products and accessories for pets.

3.

4.

5.

6.

Apple

Consumer electronics manufacturer, USA
Regis McKenna Advertising, USA, 1977; updated 1999

From the Bible to Sir Isaac Newton and beyond, the humble apple has left an indelible imprint on science, history and popular culture. Today, it is nigh on impossible to imagine our cultural landscape without the presence of one particularly high-tech apple. When Steve Jobs, Steve Wozniak and Ronald Wayne founded Apple Inc. in 1976, personal computing was in its infancy, and establishing a foothold in a business-computing market dominated by IBM and Microsoft wasn't easy. However, increasingly innovative products, wildly successful forays into consumer electronics and a sophisticated approach to branding have established Apple as one of the twenty-first century's best-known household names.

Apple Inc. launched in 1976 with an identity created by company co-founder Ron Wayne. The identity was driven by a distinctly hand-crafted logo depicting Newton under an apple tree, surrounded by a wreath motif and a banner introducing 'Apple Computer Inc.' Realizing the need for a mark that would reproduce more clearly, Steve Jobs approached Regis McKenna Advertising, where young art director Rob Janoff proceeded to develop a number of options. Beginning with the silhouette of an apple, Janoff's early efforts were deemed unsuccessful: in Apple's opinion they looked more like cherry tomatoes than apples. Unperturbed, Janoff took a bite from the apple, a simple evolution that suggested both a sense of scale and the nature of Apple's business: a play on 'bytes' and an iconic brand was born.

In 1999, the rainbow stripes introduced to advertise the launch of the Apple 2's new colour screen were removed, leaving a more simplified, versatile and sophisticated silhouette. Over the past decade, this instantly recognizable mark has proved a vital tool, helping to establish Apple as a global brand synonymous with the innovative products – most notably the iPod, iPhone and iPad – that have broadened the scope, application and accessibility of personal computing and home/personal technologies.

1.

2.

3.

4.

1. **Damloran Co.** veterinary, Iran
Ebrahim Haghighi, Iran, 1982
The symbol for a company specializing in
veterinary medicine has a strong bovine character.
2. **Ricardo Fayos** textiles, Spain
Ernesto Moradell Catalá, Spain, 1968
A ram or goat reflects a business dealing with
wool and leather.

3. **Koç Holding** conglomerates, Turkey
Chermayeff & Geismar, USA, 1984
A distinctive symbol for Turkey's largest
conglomerate: a Fortune Global 500 corporation
comprising 98 consolidated companies.
4. **Maruhachi Floss** textiles, Japan.
Katsuichi Ito Design Office, Japan, 1983
Symbol for a brand specializing in woollen
bedclothes.

5. **Polsecco** restaurants, Japan
Good Design Company, Japan, 2004
Symbol hinting at the menu of an Italian
restaurant in Tokyo's Shibuya-ku district.
6. **Halo Safet** food and beverages, Denmark
Armada d.o.o., Slovenia, 2007
This symbol is part of the identity for a chef
known for traditional Balkan specialities such
as barbecued pork.

5.

6.

7.

8.

9.

10.

11.

12.

13.

14.

7. **NETTO** retail, Denmark
Peter Hiort, Denmark, 1991
A Scottish terrier with a shopping basket in its
mouth sets a playful tone while communicating
notions of value and trust in this symbol for a
supermarket chain with stores in Denmark,
Gemany and the UK.

8. **For The Dogs** retail, Canada
Concrete Design, Canada, 2007
A roughly drawn dog supports the vibrant
personality of a brand selling canine fashion
accessories.

9. **Trussardi** fashion, Italy
Method Inc, USA, 2007
The symbol refines the fashion brand's venerable
greyhound, modernizing its shape and structure
while remaining sensitive to its historical pedigree.

10. **The Bulldog Trust** charity, UK
Mytton Williams Ltd, UK, 2008–09
Symbol for a charitable trust that provides
financial and advisory assistance to charities.

11. **The Dogs** sport and leisure, Ireland
Creative Inc., Ireland, 2005
Mark symbolizing the colours, patterns and
designs worn by racing greyhounds; it was
designed for the Irish Greyhound Board.

12. **Invest Smart** finance, Australia
THERE, Australia, 2008
A confident image for a company providing
Australian retail investors with low-cost access
to quality financial information and products.

13. **Cine Español** arts and culture, Argentina
Boldrini & Ficcardi, Argentina, 2000
This symbol, often set against a red background,
ensures there is no mistaking the Spanish flavour
of this film festival.

14. **Merrill Lynch** finance, USA
King-Casey, USA, 1972–74
Inspired by an advertisement that featured a herd
of cattle, the bull identifies one of the world's
leading financial management and advisory
companies as 'A Breed Apart'.

15.

15. **GSR: The Ghan** transport/travel, Australia
Cato Partners, Australia, 2007
Symbol for one of Australia's four great train
journeys. The Ghan links Adelaide and Darwin
via Alice Springs – hence the desert imagery.

16. **LOBEZ Powiatowa Stadnina Ogierów**
horse breeding, Poland
Karol Sliwka, Poland, 1991
Symbol for a stud farm specializing in 'country
horse stallions'.

17. **Maddoux-Wey Arabians** horse breeding, USA
Macnab Design, USA, 1985
A play on the yin and yang symbol conveys the
nature of the business with grace and subtlety.

18. **Hästens** manufacturing, Sweden
Stockholm Design Lab, Sweden, 2001
An iconic equine symbol for one of Sweden's best
known and historic bed brands.

19. **Unbridled** sport and leisure, USA
Essex Two, USA, 2006
The name and illustrative symbol designed for a
private yacht suggest a sense of freedom.

20. **Bluewater** retail, UK
Minale Tattersfield, UK, 1999
The symbol for one of the UK's landmark retail
and leisure developments employs an illustration
of Invicta (the horse on the Kent coat of arms)
leaping out of water, connecting Bluewater to its
surrounding area and giving it roots and heritage.

21. **Taymouth** hospitality, UK
Glazer, UK, 2006
Inspired by a painting at Taymouth Castle, Scotland,
the mounted knight was part of an identity designed
to promote a 'seven-star' hotel to luxury hotel
operators and investors.

16.

17.

10.

10.

20.

21.

WWF

Charity, international
Sir Peter Scott, UK, 1961;
modified by Samenwerkende Ontwerpers bv,
The Netherlands, 2000

Officially founded as the World Wildlife Fund in 1961, the WWF was established amid fears that habitat destruction and hunting would bring about the extinction of much of Africa's wildlife. The change of name in 1986 reflected a broadening of its scope, which now encompasses all corners of the globe. With five million supporters around the world, WWF has done much to raise public awareness of issues regarding the conservation, research and restoration of the environment. Among the organization's founders were the renowned biologist Sir Julian Huxley (1887–1975) and the respected naturalist and painter Sir Peter Scott (1909–89), who designed the WWF's original panda symbol in 1961.

From the start, Scott's panda symbol has been inextricably linked to the organization. Designed in black and white so it could be easily copied and recognized throughout the world, Scott's symbol has been updated several times – most recently in 2000 – and yet it retains the character and warmth that distinguished his very first design. An Olympic yachtsman, America's Cup captain, a popular TV presenter, a gliding champion and holder of the Distinguished Service Cross for Gallantry, Scott achieved a great deal during his lifetime. By designing the WWF symbol, he made a contribution to the protection of wildlife and the environment that continues to this day.

The WWF logo always comprises both the panda symbol and the WWF name: they are only ever used in application together. We are grateful to the WWF for making an exception on this occasion.

WWF researcher monitoring a coral reef in the Sulu Sea, Tubbataha reef, Philippines.

Conservation: WWF international staff monitor logging operations in Gabon, Central Africa.

WWF researcher with newly hatched sea turtles, Turtle Island, Philippines.

Antonoia Muzuma playing a game of cards to teach about conservation, Otijkavare village, Ehi-rovipuka Conservancy, Kunene, Namibia.

Mbiwo Constantine Kusebahasa, WWF Climate Witness, buying pine tree saplings to plant on his land. WWF has helped 574 farmers in the region plant 700,000 trees in its 5-year programme to replenish the bare hills. Kasese, Rwenzori Mountains, Uganda.

WWF protesters at the candlelit vigil outside the Bella Centre at the end of 'The World Wants a Real Deal' Global Day of Action march, 12 December 2009 in Copenhagen, COP 15, United Nations Climate Change Conference, Copenhagen, Denmark.

WWF protesters at the fourteenth United Nations Climate Change Conference, December 2008, Poznan, Poland.

1.

2.

3.

4.

5.

6.

7.

8.

9.

10.

11.

1. **Lof der Zoetheld** restaurants, The Netherlands
Eva Lindeman graphic design & illustration, The Netherlands, 2008
A contemporary take on the great Russian 'bear', for a Russian tea room in Rotterdam.

2. **Pola Honora** water purification, Croatia
Likovni Studio, Croatia, 1999
The ancient symbol of Uroboros, the snake, eating its own tail symbolizes recycling, renewal and purification.

3. **Hasenbichler GmbH** air conditioning, Austria
Modelhart Design, Austria, 1996
A refreshed, leaping hare represents a supplier of refrigeration and air-conditioning services.

4. **Frog** education, UK
10 Associates, UK, 2007
A playful character identifies the UK's most advanced secondary learning platform.

5. **Pochin** property development, UK
Funnel Creative, UK, 2001
A warm but industrious elephant suggests the strength and integrity of a growing business group.

6. **Ursos Lusos** non-profit organizations, Portugal
Bürocratik, Portugal, 2004
An Iberian brown bear (Ursus Arctos) symbolizes the 'bear' subculture of Portugal's gay community.

7. **Nizuc** property, Mexico
Carbone Smolan Agency, USA, 2006
This anthropomorphic character expresses the unique spirit and Mayan heritage of an exclusive Mexican resort.

8. **Australian Grown** trade, Australia
Cato Partners, Australia, 2007
A simplified yet unmistakably Australian icon is used to promote home-grown produce.

9. **Qantas Airways Limited** transport, Australia
Hulsbosch Communications, Australia, 2007
A dynamic redesign of the airline's iconic kangaroo (designed by Tony Lunn Design Group), which was used for 23 years. The launch of this sleeker, reinvigorated symbol coincided with the arrival of Qantas's new A380 aircraft.

10. **California Conservation Corp** non-profit organizations, USA
Vanderbyl Design, USA, 1978
A bear and her cub support the CCC's mission to protect California's natural beauty from fire, flood and other disasters.

11. **Fjällräven** clothing and accessories, Sweden
Fjällräven, Sweden, c.1974
Swedish for 'mountain fox', *Fjällräven* is a manufacturer of outdoors clothing and rucksacks.

12.

13.

14.

15.

16.

17.

18.

19.

20.

12. Gemeinde Rechberghausen
municipality, Germany
*Büro Uebele Visuelle Kommunikation,
Germany, 2004*
Inspired by the German town's coat of arms,
this dynamic roebuck presents a warm yet
professional image.
13. Elk Bar hospitality, UK
Zip Design, UK, 2008
A simple silhouette design for a popular bar,
part of the Mint Group, in Fulham, west London.

14. NAF automotive, Norway
Mission Design, Norway, 2006
A revitalized symbol for the Norwegian
Automobile Association expresses the core
concept of mobility.
15. Giant Generator entertainment, Austria
Q2 Design, Austria, 2003
A distinguished and distinctly modern lion.

16. Koninklijke Nederlandse Voetbalbond
sport and leisure, The Netherlands
Samenwerkende Ontwerpers, The Netherlands, 1998
A lion suggests the country's proud heritage
in this symbol for the Royal Netherlands Football
Association.
17. ShoSho sport and leisure, South Africa
Mister Walker, South Africa, 2008
Symbol for Shosholozo, which aims to create
a single iconic sports brand 'owned' by all
South Africans.

21.

18. International Film Festival Rotterdam
events, The Netherlands
75B, The Netherlands, 2008
The new identity for a prestigious film festival
updates the appearance of its mascot, a tiger.

19. Werribee Open Range Zoo tourism, Australia
David Lancashire Design, Australia, 2002
A pair of zebras evokes the exotic qualities
and attractions of a savannah-themed zoo
near Melbourne.

20. Zepra restaurants, Israel
Koniak Design, Israel, 2007
This symbol illustrates two Hebrew words –
zipor (bird) and *zepra* (zebra) – which, to the
restaurant's Israeli clientele, suggest a culinary
blend of East and West.

21. World Environmental Day environmental
advocacy/events, Japan
Ken Miki & Associates, Japan, 1999
A cornucopia of flora and fauna communicates
the focus of a United Nations Environment
Programme.

The New York
Public Library

Libraries, USA
The New York Public Library, USA, 2009

One of the world's leading public and research libraries, The New York Public Library (NYPL) has a proud and distinguished heritage. The physical embodiment of that pride and heritage are Fortitude and Patience, the two lion sculptures guarding the library's main entrance. Having provided the inspiration for the NYPL's existing symbol, Fortitude and Patience were again called upon when in-house art director Marc Blaustein and his team set about updating the library's image.

The fine detail of the existing symbol had long proved difficult to reproduce at smaller scales, so the designers set about simplifying the forms, drawing myriad interpretations of the lion's head before finding the most dynamic and evocative composition.

Identifying the need to convey a more digital-friendly, modern tone, the in-house team looked at stained glass, Japanese woodcuts and old printers' marks for inspiration. The final design evokes this sense of heritage but also conveys a fresh, forward-thinking tone, complementing the humanist qualities of the new house typeface, Kievit.

And so the lions live on, but is the new mark modeled on Fortitude or Patience? According to Blaustein, the new symbol is based primarily on Fortitude: 'The angle is Fortitude, but some of the features are inspired by Patience.'

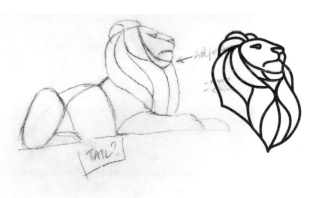

FINAL

Stills from a promotional video for the launch of the new symbol, 2009.

1.

2.

3.

4.

5.

6.

7.

8.

9.

10.

11.

12.

13.

14.

1. **Galanteria Drewna** manufacturing, Poland
   Emilia Nozko-Paprocka, Poland, 1967
   A playful mark for a manufacturer of wooden toys.
2. **Mission Festival** events/religion, Finland
   Kari Piippo, Finland, 2004
   A suitably peaceful symbol for a religious festival.
3. **Israel Week at Bloomingdale's** retail, USA
   Dan Reisinger, Israel, 1979
   Symbol designed to promote a celebration of
   Jewish culture at the famous New York
   department store.
4. **Bluebird Café** restaurants, USA
   Design Ranch, USA, 2003
   A playful symbol for a vegetarian restaurant
   in Kansas City, Missouri.
5. **The Yardbird** hospitality, UK
   Clusta, UK, 2007
   An edgy, illustrative 'yardbird' suggests the spirit
   of a live music venue in Birmingham.

6. **Allegro Film** film, Austria
   Buero X Vienna, Austria, 1998
   A playful, illustrative symbol for an Austrian
   cinema and television film-production company.
7. **Concrest** hospitality, USA
   The Brothers Bogusky, USA, 1975
   Stylized bird motif for a hotel in the Florida Keys.
8. **Booksellers' Organizations** retail, international
   Erik Ellegaard Frederiksen, Denmark, 1969
   A wise owl for booksellers' organizations in
   Denmark, Sweden and Switzerland. The designer
   is perhaps best known for his work with Jan
   Tschichold at Penguin in the 1950s.
9. **New England Farms Packing Company**
   food and beverages, USA
   BrandEquity, USA, 1976
   A distinctive rooster reinforces the fresh-food
   promise of the client's business: 'Picked before
   the rooster crows'.
10. **Robin, Inc.** manufacturing, USA
    The Brothers Bogusky, USA, 1985
    A stylized bird with a length of thread in its
    beak in this symbol for a sewing supplies brand.

11. **Iran Baby Food Industries** food and
    beverages, Iran
    Ebrahim Haghighi, Iran, 1983
    A peaceful bird and chick symbol suggests
    nurturing.
12. **Cheyenne Mountain Ranch** property
    development, USA
    Denis Parkhurst, USA, 1975
    Symbol for a residential and business
    development on a meadow plateau below
    the Rocky Mountains.
13. **Freedom 55 Financial** insurance, Canada
    Gottschalk+Ash International, Canada, 2001
    A bird of freedom suggests the perks provided by
    an insurance and retirement investment scheme
    founded by London Life.
14. **Qoqnous** publishing, Iran
    Ebrahim Haghighi, Iran, 1980
    A stylized phoenix (*qoqnous* in Persian).

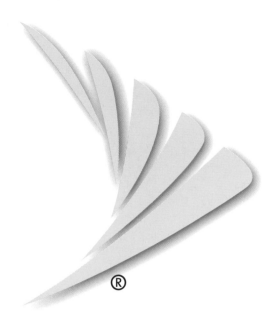

Sprint

Telecoms, USA
Lippincott, USA, 2006

The Sprint Nextel Corporation – parent company of the Sprint telecoms brand – was formed when Sprint Corporation acquired Nextel Communications in 2005, its mission: to become the USA's premier communications company. Offering a comprehensive range of wireless and 'wireline' services, it brings 'freedom of mobility to consumers, businesses and government users' and is highly regarded as an innovative brand.

Following the merger, Sprint Nextel invited Lippincott to look at its identity. While it was agreed that Sprint's broad market awareness and history of innovation made its name the natural choice for the new venture, it was decided that the identity should also celebrate Nextel's entrepreneurial spirit and expertise in instant communications.

Having identified the need to integrate the most valuable assets of each company, Lippincott brought together Sprint's signature pin-drop symbol, which represents clarity ('You can hear a pin drop'), and the dynamic qualities of Nextel's yellow and black colour palette. When it came to redesigning Sprint's pin drop, Lippincott had to bear in mind the competitive, saturated nature of the telecoms industry in the age of the Internet, mobile/cellular phones and PDAs. The new, wing-like pin-drop symbol succeeds in expressing a sense of motion and flight, evoking the dynamic and innovative values promoted by the new brand.

15.

16.

17.

18.

19.

20.

15. Firma Kosmetyczna health and beauty, Poland
Karol Sliwka, Poland, 1966
A simplified swan expresses the elegance
of a Polish cosmetics brand.

16. Hirwell clothing and accessories, Italy
Martin Diethelm, Italy, date unknown
A tranquil swan conveys the delicate quality
of this brand's hosiery.

17. Lebed unknown, Bulgaria
Stefan Kanchev, Bulgaria, c.1960–70s
An elegantly stylized swan.

18. Heron Automobiltechnik automotive, Germany
Büro Ink, Germany, 2006
A suitably bird-like mark for a company
specializing in the development of performance-
enhancing technologies.

19. GSR: The Overland transport/travel, Australia
Cato Partners, Australia, 2007
An emu symbolizes one of Australia's four great
train journeys; the Overland links Adelaide and
Melbourne.

20. Penguin military, Italy
Studio FM Milano, Italy, 2000
A sentient penguin motif sets an intelligent tone
for this naval project-planning agency.

21.

22.

23.

24.

25.

26.

21. **Azady Hotel** hospitality, Iran
Ebrahim Haghighi, Iran, 1983
An elegant dove symbolizes the meaning of the
hotel's name (*azady* is Persian for freedom).

22. **Bonving-Skofabrik** textiles, Sweden
Fritjof Pedersen, Sweden, date unknown
Symbol for a manufacturer of fibres.

23. **Sandpiper** hospitality, USA
The Brothers Bogusky, USA, 1979
A stylized bird suggests the natural beauty
of a hotel on Florida's west coast.

24. **Ambaba** retail, UK
Graphical House, UK, 2008
A warm, playful symbol for a childrenswear brand.

25. **Falcon International** film, USA
Gips & Dannel, USA, date unknown
A proud falcon on a celluloid strip conveys both
the name and focus of the business.

26. **Ministerstwo Lacznosci** telecoms, Poland
Karol Sliwka, Poland, 1975–76
The bird symbolizes communicating
across great distances.

27.

28.

29.

30.

27. Shreveport Management Consultancy
consultancy, UK
To The Point Ltd, UK, 2002
Arrows representing flying geese support
this company's belief in good management –
the ultimate team effort, these birds rotate in
V formation to take pressure off the leader.

28. TACA Airlines transport, El Salvador
Lippincott, USA, 2008
An exotic bird symbolizes flight and destinations
for an airline flying to over 39 locations across
the Americas.

29. UK Presidency of Europe 2005 government, EU
johnson banks, UK, 2004
The presidency of Europe changes every six
months and swans take it in turns to fly at the head
of their formation – hence this avian solution
marking the UK's term.

30. Kongres Swiatowej Rady Pokoju events, Poland
Karol Sliwka, Poland, 1987
Stylized doves suggest the peaceful union of
countries at an international congress held in
Poland.

31.

32.

31. NBC (National Broadcasting Company)
broadcasting, USA
Chermayeff & Geismar, USA, 1985
The NBC peacock first appeared on American
TV screens in 1956. While dignified, distinctive,
light-hearted and memorable, it was never
adopted as the company's official logo. In 1985
NBC launched a new and strikingly simple
peacock, which has since become one of the
world's most recognizable trademarks.

32. Lufthansa transport, Germany
Otto Firle, Germany, 1918; modified by Otl Aicher,
Germany, 1969
The first 'crane' symbol was designed by
Professor Otto Firle for Germany's first airline,
Deutsche Luftreederei GmbH (DLR). Clean and
modern, the symbol survived several mergers and
was retained in the late 1960s when Deutsche Luft
Hansa AG, the company created as a result of
those mergers, appointed Otl Aicher to review its
identity. Aicher gave the crane a more streamlined
appearance, thereby consolidating the themes of
flight and technical skill that have always been
central to the Lufthansa brand. By placing the
refreshed crane in a circle and introducing a new
Helvetica Bold logotype, Aicher had raised the bar,
his work for Lufthansa proving to be a lasting
influence on the art and craft of modern
corporate identity design.

Penguin

Penguin Publishing, UK
Edward Young, UK, 1935; modified by Jan Tschichold, 1946, and Pentagram, UK, 2003

A director at publishing house Bodley Head, Allen Lane (1902–70) was returning from a weekend at Agatha Christie's when he decided to buy a book for the journey home. Appalled by the selection of magazines and reprinted Victorian novels available on the station news-stand, he decided to make high-quality contemporary fiction available at an attractive price by introducing paperbacks for sale in railway stations and tobacconists, as well as in bookshops. Seeking a 'dignified but flippant' symbol for his new venture, Lane asked his secretary for ideas. Her suggestion of a penguin clearly hit the spot, as Lane asked another employee – office junior Edward Young (1913–2003) – to sketch the penguins at London Zoo.

Penguin Books was founded in 1935 and its first titles appeared in the summer of that year. Colour coded orange for fiction, blue for biographies and green for crime, they were priced at 6d (sixpence), the same price as a packet of cigarettes. Seventy years on, Penguin is one of publishing's truly iconic brands, with a wide range of merchandise from mugs and T-shirts to shopping bags and deck-chairs, complementing an innovative and celebrated publishing programme.

1935

1937

1946

2003

1959

2003

The symbol has changed slightly over the years. A redrawn version was introduced in 1946 by pioneering German-born designer Jan Tschichold (1902–74). One of several design luminaries to have worked with Penguin, he also oversaw the design of 500 paperbacks and introduced his typographic guidelines, the Penguin Composition Rules. Tschichold's symbol was retained for over half a century, but was applied inconsistently; this, and a desire to propel the publishing house into a twenty-first century dominated by the Internet, prompted Penguin's parent company Pearson PLC to appoint Pentagram to refresh the symbol and provide guidelines for its consistent usage.

As part of the same project, Pentagram redesigned the symbol for Puffin, a Penguin imprint launched in 1940 and the English-speaking world's leading publisher of children's books. Markedly different from its predecessor, the new symbol recognizes Puffin's heritage, but now bears a stronger resemblance to its ornithological roots. Combined with a new lozenge and colour, the new softer, more curvilinear design ties it much more strongly to the Penguin brand. Smart and confident, the personality of this superbly drawn symbol reflects the attitude and values that distinguish Puffin from its competitors.

33.

34.

35.

36.

37.

38.

39.

40.

41.

42.

33. **GSR: Indian Pacific** transport/travel, Australia
Cato Partners, Australia, 2007
Australia's Wedge-tailed Eagle, the biggest
eagle on earth, symbolizes one of Australia's
four great train journeys. the India Pacific links
Sydney and Perth.

34. **Outward Bound Center for Peacebuilding**
education, USA
Pentagram, USA, 2007
A stencilled dove of peace for an education
initiative working in areas of conflict.

35. **St. Joe Company** property development, USA
Chermayeff & Geismar, USA, 1998
A stylized bird suggests the natural beauty
synonymous with this land development
company in Florida.

36. **Sanquin** healthcare, The Netherlands
Total Identity Amsterdam bv, The Netherlands, 1998
A stylized pelican for a manufacturer of blood
grouping and immune reagents. In medieval
Europe, pelicans were thought to feed blood to
their young when no other food was available.

37. **THS** finance, UK
SomeOne, UK, 2008
The symbol for a London investment-fund
management company employs a visual
metaphor; hummingbirds feed only on the
nectar of selected flowers.

38. **Falck A/S** salvage company, Denmark
Bysted, Denmark, 1994
An evocative falcon reflects the company
name (also the name of its founder). Originally
designed in 1931, the symbol has since been
refreshed by Bysted.

39. **Biblioteka Pokoju** libraries, Poland
Karol Sliwka, Poland, 1987
Symbol suggesting books and the liberating
experience of learning.

40. **Inn at Mill River** hospitality, USA
Appleton Design, USA, 1987
A swan suggests the tranquil setting and
atmosphere of a Long Island hotel.

41. **Lankabaari (Yarn Bar)** hospitality, Finland
EMMI, UK, 2007
A warm, cross-stitched symbol for a café/
knitting shop (*lankabaari* is Finnish for thread bar).
Patrons are encouraged to knit while catching up
with friends.

42. **Nestlé SA** food and beverages, Switzerland
Nestlé SA, Switzerland, 1995
Originally launched by Henri Nestlé in 1868, this
iconic symbol reflects the meaning of his name in
German: little nest (an image of which appeared
on his family crest). The symbol has been through
various reincarnations over the years, and the
current modified version was designed in-house
at Nestlé in 1995. Nestlé SA is the world's leading
nutrition, health and wellness company.
Reproduced with the kind permission of Société
des Produits Nestlé S.A.

BOAC
(British Overseas Airways Corporation)

Transport, UK
Theyre Lee-Elliot, UK, 1932

Evoking the glamour and romance of air travel's golden age, BOAC's legendary Speedbird symbol was originally designed by Theyre Lee-Elliot (1903–88) for Imperial Airways and debuted in 1932. A talented artist, illustrator and designer, Lee-Elliot went on to design posters for London Underground between 1936 and 1952, including a striking example promoting an Imperial Airways exhibition, 'The Empire's Airway', at Charing Cross Station in 1936.

The Speedbird design was simple, versatile and an effective brand ambassador, first for Imperial Airways and then for BOAC following its launch in 1939. Becoming much more prominent during BOAC's aegis, the symbol appeared on both the nose and tail fin of the airline's planes. By the 1960s the Speedbird had been enlarged and applied in gold, further embracing the glamour of air travel.

Influential and revered, the symbol enjoyed a long and prosperous life; following the advent of air-traffic control, BOAC adopted the Speedbird name as their official call sign. The symbol was even retained when BOAC merged with British European Airways to form British Airways and was not phased out until 1984, when BA launched a new look as part of their preparations for privatization.

1.

2.

3.

4.

5.

6.

7.

8.

9.

10.

11.

1. **Dolphin Square** property, UK
   ico Design Consultancy, UK, 2007
   A simple, aspirational symbol applied across all
   areas (Dolphin House, Dolphin Bar & Grill, Dolphin
   Fitness Club) of an historic and rejuvenated
   property in London. Dolphin Square is owned
   by Brookhouse Capital.
2. **Alexander Fest Verlag** publishing, Germany
   Ott + Stein, Germany, 1999
   A diving whale conjures up various literary
   references for a publisher's symbol.
3. **Snapper** transport, New Zealand
   Cato Partners, Australia, 2008
   Following London's Oyster card and Hong Kong's
   Octopus card, New Zealand's Snapper top-up
   smart card was born; the symbol reflects its name.
4. **Thinkfish** sport and leisure, Spain
   ruiz+company, Spain, 2006
   A simple fish motif made up of dots is the symbol
   for a fishing-equipment brand.

5. **Bromanodell AB** sport and leisure, Sweden
   Redmanwalking, Sweden, 2004
   A fish made of two fishing hooks represents the
   two founders of a leading fishing-tackle brand.
6. **Slavyanka** fisheries, Bulgaria
   Stefan Kanchev, Bulgaria, c.1960s–70s
   A suitably piscine symbol for a fishery.
7. **onefish twofish** retail, Australia
   Naughtyfish design, Australia, 2003
   A playful symbol designed for a retailer
   of childrenswear and maternity clothing.
8. **Milan Glavina** photography, Slovenia
   OS design studio, Slovenia, 2006
   A simple graphic device that reflects the
   experience of taking photographs beneath
   the waves.

9. **Montreal Fishing Co** fisheries, Canada
   Joseph Binder, Germany, date unknown
   A strong mark communicates the company's
   business with clarity.
10. **Mac Fisheries** retail, UK
    Hans Schleger, UK, 1952–59
    Between 1952 and 1959 the legendary designer
    Hans Schleger, or Zero, designed several versions
    of the Mac Fisheries symbol – modifications of
    the original fish and salter symbol designed in
    1919. The incarnation shown here is arguably his
    definitive take on the traditional mark; the fish
    are swimming west, as always, albeit in a more
    modern manner.
11. **Sadala (Bourgas)** retail/sport and leisure,
    Bulgaria
    Stefan Kanchev, Bulgaria, c.1960s–70s
    Symbol for a fishing-equipment brand.

12.

13.

14.

15.

16.

17.

18.

19.

20.

21.

22.

12. Thames & Hudson publishing, UK
The Partners, UK, 1999
In this mark for one of the UK's leading art
publishers, founded in London and New York
in 1949, the dolphins symbolize the Thames
and Hudson rivers, as well as friendship and
intelligence working together as one.

13. Kuopio Congregation religion, Finland
Kari Piippo, Finland, 2001
Familiar Christian iconography with a modern
twist: Kuopio is also known for its association
with a national delicacy, fish pastry.

14. Luckyfish restaurants, USA
Pentagram, USA, 2008
Elegant mark for a conveyor-belt sushi restaurant
in Los Angeles.

15. Hamedan International Short Film Festival
arts and culture/events, Iran
Ebrahim Haghighi, Iran, 1986
A simple shell motif with film-reel detailing for
an annual film festival in one of the world's
oldest cities.

16. Unisuper finance, New Zealand
Cato Partners, Australia, 1999
A pearl in a shell is readily understood as
a precious asset that grows over time.

17. New England Aquarium aquarium, USA
Chermayeff & Geismar, USA, 1969
Simplicity and clarity provide an aquarium with
a bold, modern identity.

18. Silver Squid Internet, UK
Bürocratik, Portugal, 2006
From organic to pixel, this symbol is a play on
the name and business of a London-based web-
development agency.

19. Moby-Dick Wharf Restaurant restaurants, USA
Alexander Isley Inc., USA, 1993
Symbol alluding to the literary heritage associated
with the restaurant's name and location.

20. National Aquarium in Baltimore aquarium, USA
Chermayeff & Geismar, USA, 1980
Chermayeff & Geismar has been invited to
design symbols for aquariums all over the world.
These share common characteristics as each one
interprets a familiar subject in a fresh and distinctive
manner.

**21. Oceanario de Lisboa (Lisbon
Aquarium)** aquarium, Portugal
Chermayeff & Geismar, USA, 1996
A vibrant symbol for a groundbreaking
oceanarium, one of Lisbon's most popular
tourist attractions.

22. Tennessee Aquarium aquarium, USA
Chermayeff & Geismar, USA, 1999
Symbol suggesting the variety of fish, birds
and reptiles found at this Tennessee attraction.

Shell

Energy, The Netherlands
Raymond Loewy, USA, 1971; modified 1995

Today, Shell is a global group of energy and petrochemical companies whose aim is to 'meet the energy needs of society, in ways that are economically, socially and environmentally viable, now and in the future'. Sounds ambitious, but seeing as Shell's business began in an antique and bric-a-brac shop in London, it is fair to say that ambition has played a significant role in Shell's development.

The owner of that small London shop, Marcus Samuel, began his career in the 1830s selling trinkets and boxes made with exotic shells imported from the Far East. On his death in 1870, Samuel's son – also called Marcus – maintained the company's connections with the Orient and in 1878 co-founded Marcus Samuel and Company. During the 1880s and 1890s the business focused on importing and exporting oil and in 1897 changed its name to Shell Transport and Trading Ltd, having previously adopted the word 'shell' as a trademark on boxes of kerosene bound for the Far East. In 1901 the company adopted a mussel shell as its trademark and then, three years later, the mussel shell changed to a scallop, or pecten, shell, and an iconic identity was born.

In 1907, Shell Transport and Trading merged with the Royal Dutch Petroleum Company, but its name and pecten motif were retained. The symbol has morphed slightly over the years, but Shell seems to have settled, rather wisely, on the timeless version designed by Raymond Loewy in 1971. New, brighter colours were introduced in 1995, but the basic visual form of the shell remains true to Loewy's precise and well-balanced motif. This is complemented by a striking palette, the history of which harks back to California, where Shell started to open service stations in 1915. Deciding that a bright colour palette would help distinguish it from the competition, it settled on red and yellow, the colours of the Spanish flag, reflecting the state's connections with Spain.

1900

1904

1909

1930

1948

1955

1961

1971

1995

1999

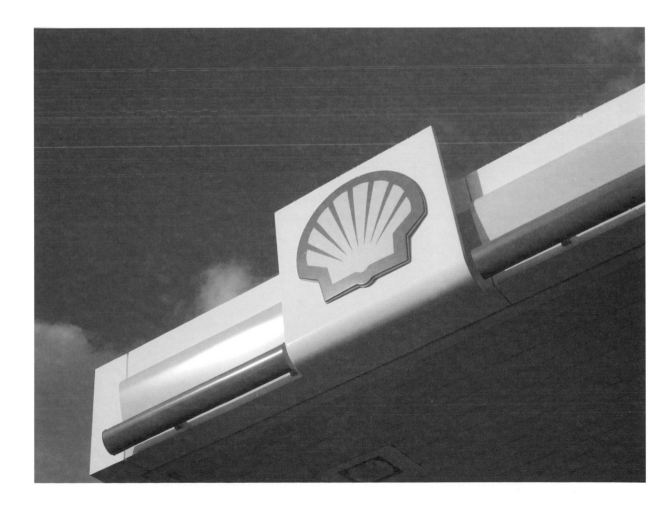

1.

2.

3.

4.

5.

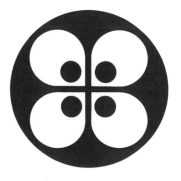

6.

7.

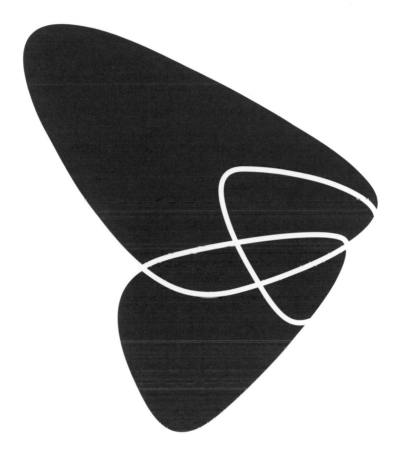

1. **IV Festival Internacional de Buenos Aires**
    arts and culture/events, Argentina
    Bernardo + Celis, Argentina, 2003
    A vibrant butterfly brings a celebratory tone
    to a promotional identity.
2. **Clairia** manufacturing, Finland
    Porkka & Kuutsa, Finland, 2003
    A butterfly represents clean, fresh air in this
    symbol for a manufacturer of air filters for
    industrial and commercial use.

3. **SK Group** conglomerates, South Korea
    Lippincott, USA, 2005
    Soaring wings illustrate the progressive nature,
    commitment to innovation, high standards and
    global reach of South Korea's third-largest
    conglomerate.
4. **Irish Silk Poplin** textiles, Ireland
    Louis le Brocquy and D. Litt, Ireland, date unknown
    A stylized moth recalls the natural source of silk.
5. **R. Murray & Son Ltd. Bayberry Estates**
    property development, Canada
    Raymond Lee, Canada, 1970
    Symbol conveying the natural beauty of a housing
    development in Toronto.

6. **Chrysalis** music, UK
    Bostock and Pollitt, UK, 2003
    A simplified look for the media group's famous
    butterfly symbol refreshes its identity.
7. **Votiva** finance, Australia
    THERE, Australia, 2008
    A stylized butterfly supports the client's aim to
    make a positive difference to people's lives, with
    practices based on sound business ethics,
    courtesy and support.

8.

8. **Elevance** science, USA
    Addis Creson, USA, 2008
    The hexagon symbolizes chemistry, and the
    infinity sign suggests sustainability, while the bee
    symbolizes teamwork and productivity for this
    renewable sciences company.

9. **Krefina Bank** finance, Switzerland
    Robert Geisser, Switzerland, date unknown
    A simplified bee indicates an industrious brand,
    and the accumulation and storage of wealth.

10. **Nektarcoop** cooperatives, Bulgaria
    Ŝtefan Kanchev, Bulgaria, c.1960s–70s
    A beautifully simple bee and honeycomb
    surround suggests industry and cooperation.

11. **British Bee Society** charity, UK
    Peter Grundy, UK, 1995
    Simple geometric shapes combine to create
    the unmistakable form of a bumblebee.

12. **Manchester Credit Union** finance, UK
    Funnel Creative, UK, 2007
    A hand-drawn bee refers to Manchester's
    industrious heritage and a city mascot that is
    growing in popularity.

9.

10.

11.

12.

1.

2.

3.

4.

5.

6.

7.

8.

1. **Pegasus Luggage** manufacturing, USA
The Brothers Bogusky, USA, 1981
Crafted, aspirational mark for a manufacturer of fine luggage.
2. **Welsh Development Agency** public services, UK
Glazer, UK, 2003
The dragon draws on patriotic iconography for a brand encompassing a wide range of economic activities.
3. **West Point Pepperell** textiles, USA
Lippincott, USA, 1988
Engaging symbol for a leading textile manufacturer, now part of the West Point Home conglomerate.

4. **Prehm & Arendt** food and beverages, Germany
Bionic Systems, Germany, 2000
This symbol for a wine wholesaler adopts the lion from Düsseldorf's coat of arms and presents him with a box of wine – this way up!
5. **National Botanic Garden of Wales** arts and culture, UK
Pentagram, UK, 1997
A Welsh dragon and leaf motif designed for a botanical garden in Dyfed.
6. **Mobil Corporation** energy, USA
Chermayeff & Geismar, USA, 1964
The iconic Pegasus symbol is a modernized version of the mark adopted by Socony-Vacuum in 1931. Socony-Vacuum became the Mobil Oil Corporation in 1966. The symbol is no longer in use.

7. **The Asia Society** non-profit organizations, USA
Pentagram, USA, 1997
Mark for an organization promoting awareness of Asian culture. The leogryph symbol (combining a lion and griffin) has meaning across many Asian cultures.
8. **Beijing 2008** sport and leisure, Finland
Hahmo, Finland, 1996
Symbol representing and promoting Amnesty International's Finnish representation at the 2008 Olympics in Beijing.

1.

2.

3.

4.

5.

6.

7.

8.

1. **Clear Capital** finance, USA
   Method Inc., USA, 2008
   A revitalized mark for one of the USA's leading
   providers of loan valuations.
2. **Housing & Sport Network** community
   initiatives, UK
   Slingshot, UK, 2009
   Symbol for an organization working to improve
   partnerships between housing and sport
   sectors in the development of community-based
   sports projects.
3. **Industrieverband Agrar** professional
   association, Germany
   Stankowski + Duschek, Germany, 1999
   Private industrial association of 47 companies
   in the agricultural sector.

4. **Airfields of Britain Conservation Trust**
   charity, UK
   Remedy, UK, 2006
   The trust was created to help save Britain's
   historic airfields for generations to come.
5. **Invesco Fund Managers Ltd** finance, UK
   Browns Design, UK, 2007
   A modern reinterpretation of a mountain symbol
   once used by Perpetual, who merged with Invesco
   in 2000. This is part of a global identity programme
   for one of the world's largest investment
   managers.

6. **Filmandes** events/film, Argentina
   Boldrini & Ficcardi, Argentina, 2000
   Symbol for a festival celebrating filmmakers from
   countries along the Andes range.
7. **Monier** construction, Germany
   Coley Porter Bell, UK, 2008
   An illustrative landscape for the 'world leader
   in quality roofing' suggests their specialism.
8. **Aeropuerto Regional** transport, Argentina
   Fileni & Fileni Design, Argentina, 1998
   A curved and mountainous landscape conveys
   both a view from the air and the wings of an
   aeroplane.

9.

10.

11.

12.

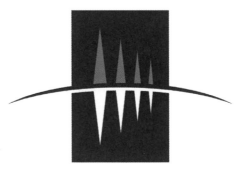

9. **Minerals Ireland** exploration/mining, Ireland
Dara Creative, Ireland, 2008
A simple mark suggesting landscape and the
bounty found beneath its surface.

10. **Machare Kilimanjaro** food and beverages,
Tanzania
Tisch Eins, Germany, 2004
A mountain scene provides an evocative icon
for a luxury coffee brand.

11. **Hawkshead** clothing and accessories, UK
FOUR IV, UK, 2003
A mountainous landscape implies the terrain
enjoyed by wearers of garments by this casual
and countryside clothing label.

12. **Umhlanga Ridge New Town Centre** property
development, South Africa
Mister Walker, South Africa, 1997
Symbol communicating the natural beauty of a
new and expansive development outside Durban.

13. **Dutch Ministry of LNV** government,
The Netherlands
Studio Dumbar, The Netherlands, 1986
A landscape illustrates the remit of Holland's
Ministry of Agriculture, Nature Management
and Food Quality.

14. **Coworth Park** hospitality, UK
& SMITH, UK, 2009
Avoiding visual cliché, this contemporary symbol
supports the creative spirit of a 'country house
hotel with a difference'. Coworth Park is a
Dorchester Collection hotel.

13.

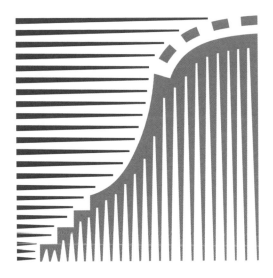

14.

1.

2.

3.

4.

5.

6.

7.

8.

9.

10.

1. **Popcorn Taxi** events, Australia
   Mark Gowing, Australia, 2006
   A playful star supports the 'watch the films, meet
   the makers' strapline of a company organizing
   live film discussion events.

2. **Montblanc International GmbH** manufacturing,
   Germany
   Lindinger Design, Germany, 1967
   This iconic symbol has helped Montblanc evolve
   from a leading manufacturer of premium writing
   instruments to a diverse brand producing luxury
   goods such as watches, leather and jewellery.

3. **Aldrich Eastman Waltch** property, USA
   Pentagram, USA, 1993–94
   Symbol for a real-estate advisory firm providing
   asset management and related services.

4. **5tar Films** film, South Africa
   Reghardt, South Africa, 2009
   A simple but effective reinterpretation of a
   reel of film carries a pictorial clue to the film
   agency's name.

5. **Surgical Design Corporation** healthcare, USA
   Danne Design, USA, 1990
   Symbol for a company that invents and produces
   high-tech instruments for cataract surgery.

6. **Chrysler Corporation** automotive, USA
   Lippincott, USA, 1962
   Iconic star symbol designed for the historic
   American car brand. It was superseded in 2010
   by a new 'wing' mark.

7. **Lifehouse at RPA** healthcare, Australia
   Cato Partners, Australia, 2008
   Five houses form a star-shaped community
   providing cancer support and research at
   the Royal Prince Alfred Hospital in Sydney.

8. **Japan Six Cities Trade Exhibition
   Association** trade, Japan
   Nishiwaki Tomoichi and Uedo Akisato, Japan, 1971
   Six forms radiate from a star, indicating the six
   cities promoted by a centre for overseas trade
   in Kyoto.

9. **London Innovation** business development, UK
   KentLyons, UK, 2003
   A lively mark for a business initiative created
   and led by the London Development Agency.

10. **A.P. Møller – Mærsk** energy/shipping, Denmark
    Acton Bjorn, Denmark, 1971
    When Captain Peter Mærsk Møller took command
    of his first steamer in 1886, the funnel was ringed
    with a blue band with a white seven-point star
    on each side; the rest is history. The current
    version was modified in 1971.

11.

12.

13.

14.

15.

16.

11. **American Republic Life Insurance Company** insurance, USA
Chermayeff & Geismar, USA, 1964
A patriotic symbol with two eagles (the size variation conveys ideas of family) forming star shapes.

12. **US Canoe & Kayak Team** sport and leisure, USA
Crosby Associates, USA, 1995
A patriotic star blends with a stylized river motif.

13. **Bahrain National Insurance (BNI)** finance, Bahrain
Unisono, Bahrain, 2007
In this vibrant mark, five bold forms rotate to create a perfect star out of negative space.

14. **Star Alliance** transport, Germany
Pentagram, UK, 1997
Symbol representing the coming together of five leading airlines; Star Alliance is now the largest of its kind with 26 members (in March 2010).

15. **Texas Biotechnology Corp** biotechnology, USA
Pentagram, USA, 1990
This symbol combines the Texas lone star and a heart for a biotechnology company specializing in cardiological research.

16. **American Film Institute** arts and culture, USA
Chermayeff & Geismar, USA, 1968
A simple, playful symbol celebrating the stars of Amercian cinema.

17.

18.

19.

20.

21.

22.

17. Blue Security security, South Africa
Mister Walker, South Africa, 2006
A distinctive police-style symbol for a
Durban-based company providing alarms
and armed-response security.

18. Climacer air conditioning, Portugal
Bürocratik, Portugal, 2004
A cool, refreshing mark for one of Portugal's
leading designers and installers of air conditioning.

19. Geo Nova sustainable products, Mexico
Manolo Fernández Oria, Mexico, 2008
A stylized sunflower suggests a source of
energy for a company providing sustainable
solutions for developers, builders, architects
and interior designers.

20. Citibox property, Poland
Logotypy.com, Poland, 2006
Six rotating boxes form a robust and
energetic star.

21. United States Bicentennial Commission
events, USA
Chermayeff & Geismar, USA, 1976
The official symbol designed to mark nationwide
celebrations of America's 200th birthday evoked
the spirit and culture of the United States.

22. Sevlievo textiles, Bulgaria
Stefan Kanchev, Bulgaria, c.1960s–70s
A woven star for a textile manufacturer.

23.

24.

25.

26.

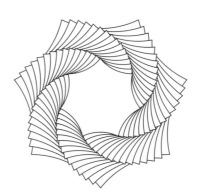

27.

28.

29.

30.

23. Sustainable architecture publishing, Belgium
Coast, Belgium, 2008
The silhouettes of houses form a mark for an
imprint of architectural publisher Prisme Editions.

24. Heyerdahl jewellers, Norway
Mission Design, Norway, 2008
A simple combination of squares creates a cluster
of gems and a modern, aspirational symbol.

25. Bahrain National Holding (BNH) finance, Bahrain
Unisono, Bahrain, 2007
Two overlapping stars suggest a sense of place
as well as strength and reliability.

26. The Chicago Spire property development, USA
Marque, UK/USA, 2007
Designed for a landmark property development
in Chicago, this symbol creates a kinetic image
incorporating both the footprint of the building
and the shells that inspired the project's architect,
Santiago Calatrava.

27. Dubai Airports transport, UAE
Cato Partners, Australia, 2000
Mark symbolizing the aviation hub of the world
through a globe comprised of ancient Middle
Eastern mosaics.

28. Bliadhna broadcasting, UK
Graphical House, UK, 2008
Vibrant symbol for a music programme to
celebrate the Gaelic new year. It illustrates seating
around a stage while also resembling a snowflake
and an exploding firework.

29. UEFA Champions League sport and leisure,
Switzerland
Design Bridge, UK, 1992
The stars represent the best teams in Europe;
a black and white palette ensures clarity in a world
of bright team colours and sponsors.

30. Commercial Bank of Kuwait finance, USA
Pentagram, UK, 1979–80
Stylized Arabic type inhabits a star emblem
designed for a consumer and corporate bank
established in 1960.

1.

2.

1. **Universal Development Corp** property development, USA
    Visual Design Center, USA, date unknown
    A stylized solar symbol indicates the climate in Arizona, where this business developed new communities.
2. **Sungevity** energy, USA
    Addis Creson, USA, 2007
    The house motif and sunlike form symbolize the shift of 'power to people' and changing for the better.
3. **Young Audiences** education, USA
    Chermayeff & Geismar, USA, 1982
    A playful sun for a non-profit organization that works with educational systems, the arts community and private and public sectors to provide arts education for children.
4. **Ring of Fire Aquarium** aquarium, Japan
    Chermayeff & Geismar, USA, 1988
    A circular body of water ringed by flames mirrors the unique name of an Osaka aquarium.

5. **Smithsonian Institute** arts and culture, USA
    Chermayeff & Geismar, USA, 1999
    Following rapid expansion, Washington's Smithsonian required a consistent and coherent image. This iconic sun symbol is a familiar sight in the city.
6. **Pacific Lighting Corporation** pharmaceuticals, USA
    Denis and Ken Parkhurst, USA, c.1970
    Symbol reflecting the corporation's name, its Pacific Coast location and the pie-chart make-up of its subsidiary companies.
7. **The Franklin Institute** arts and culture, USA
    Allemann Almquist & Jones, USA, 1989
    Bright, optimistic symbol reflecting the institute's mission to 'inspire an understanding of and passion for science and technology learning'.
8. **Skywest** transport, Australia
    Cato Partners, Australia, 2002
    The flaring sun seen through an aeroplane window is symbolized in the identity for this airline.
9. **Suncorp Metway** finance, Australia
    Cato Partners, Australia, 2004
    The sun rising on a new horizon sets an optimistic tone for one of Australia's leading financial services groups.

10. **Columbus Regional Hospital** healthcare, USA
    Pentagram, USA, 1991
    A positive vision for a new building at the Bartholomew County Hospital in Indiana.
11. **Ohio National Financial Services** finance, USA
    Pentagram, USA, 1996
    An optimistic combination of an upward-moving profit chart and a rising sun.
12. **Sun Laboratories** pharmaceuticals, China
    Tsung Yi-Lu, China, date unknown
    A stylized sun motif mirrors the name of this pharmaceuticals company.
13. **Betlemská Kaple** arts and culture, Czech Republic
    Jiří Rathouský, Czech Republic, 1967
    A vibrant symbol for an art gallery in Prague.
14. **City of Irvine, California** property development, USA
    Ken and Denis Parkhurst, USA, c.1970
    Symbol for a new city on the south California coast. Originally designed for a retail and business centre, it was later adopted to identify the overall community.

3.

4.

5.

6.

7.

8.

9.

10.

11.

12.

13.

14.

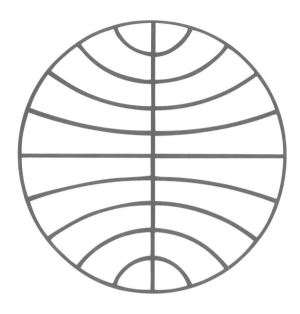

Pan Am

Transport, USA
Edward Larrabee Barnes/Charles Forberg/
Ivan Chermayeff, USA, c.1955;
redesigned by Chermayeff & Geismar, USA, 1971

Pan American World Airways was founded in 1927 as a scheduled airmail and passenger service operating between Florida and Havana. With its refined image and famous flying boats, or 'Clippers', the airline soon became synonymous with the romance and glamour of 1930s air travel. In the mid-1950s the company announced the arrival of America's first commercial jets with a revamped identity courtesy of New York architect Edward Larrabee Barnes (appointed as Pan American's consultant designer in 1955) and his associate, Charles Forberg. Barnes and Forberg in turn asked Ivan Chermayeff, then on their staff, to redesign the airline's logotype and symbol. They replaced the existing symbol, a stylized wing and globe motif, with a simplified blue globe overlaid with parabolic lines: a symbol of the drive and ambition that continued to define Pan American's pioneering spirit.

When Najeeb Halaby became chairman in 1970, his desire to breathe new life into the airline prompted an invigorating yet short-lived design programme. Patrick Friesner, Pan American's head of sales and promotion, commissioned work by the period's finest designers including George Tscherny, Rudolph de Harak and Alan Fletcher. At the core of the programme was a new visual identity designed by Chermayeff & Geismar, the most important element of which was a change of name from Pan American World Airways to Pan Am. A refreshed globe and a new logotype set in Helvetica Medium promoted a cleaner, more modern tone, with the airline's signature colour palette of royal blue still firmly in place. The most acclaimed applications of Chermayeff & Geismar's identity are the promotional poster series designed in 1971 and 1972: the marriage of evocative photography and minimal type communicates a unique and sophisticated sense of adventure.

Halaby was forced to resign in 1972, and his successors wandered away from the clarity of Chermayeff & Geismar's identity, but Pan Am retained the iconic blue globe until its demise in 1991.

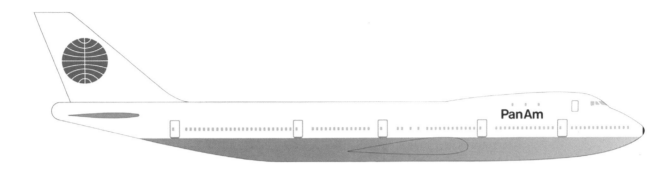

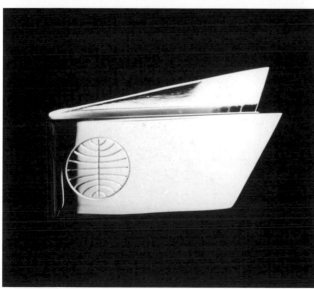

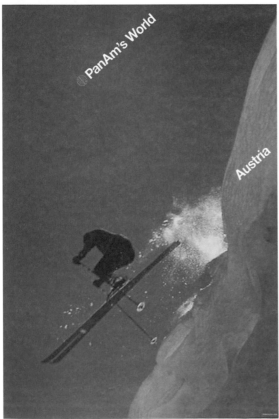

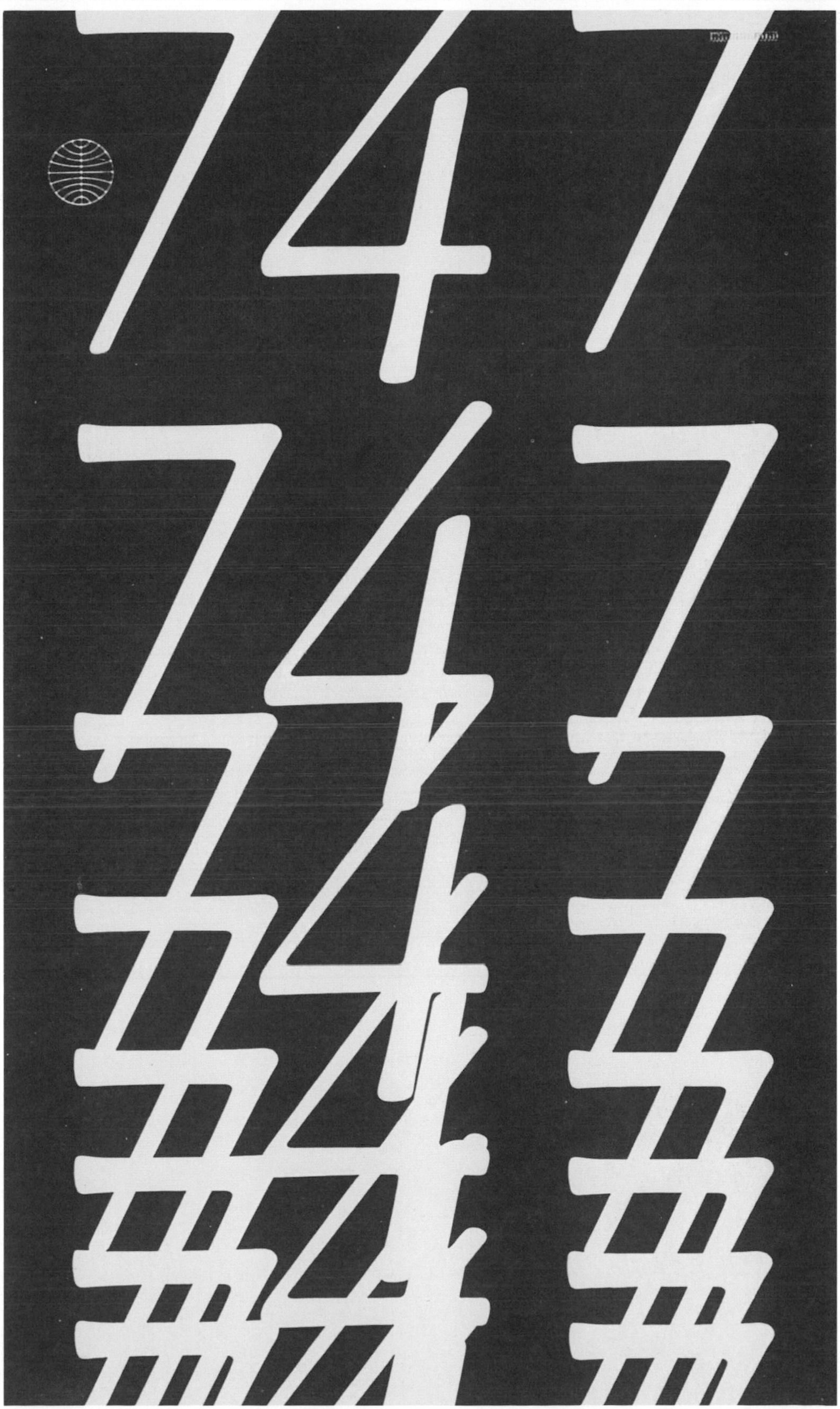
747

1.

2.

3.

4.

5.

6.

7.

8.

9.

10.

1. **Globalsounds.info** Internet, Switzerland
    Büro Destruct, Switzerland, 2009
    An appropriately global mark reflects the mission
    of a German website promoting world music.
2. **theglobe.com** Internet, USA
    Pentagram, USA, 1998
    Online social networking resource that brings
    people together around shared topics of interest.
3. **Public Radio International** broadcasting, USA
    Pentagram, USA, 1994
    Mark symbolizing the network's role as the new
    voice of world news, current events and culture.
4. **Den Norske Bank** finance, Norway
    Scandinavian Design Group, Norway, 1990
    A simple device expressing the global scope
    of a bank that merged with Gjensidige NOR in
    2003 to form DnB NOR. The mark was designed
    by Skaara & Partners, which became Scandinavian
    Design Group in 1991.

5. **ACR World** recruitment, Australia
    THERE, Australia, 2009
    A stylized globe motif for a specialist Australian
    recruitment company for expats, targeting senior
    national and international appointments.
6. **Saturn Electro-Handelsgesellschaft mbH**
    retail, Germany
    KMS TEAM, Germany, 1999
    A stylized representation of the planet Saturn
    echoes the brand name.
7. **Pfeifhofer Radsport** sport and leisure, Austria
    Modelhart Design, Austria, 2006
    A cropped circular motif suggesting turning
    wheels for a cycling shop and repair service.

8. **Hemisphere Club** restaurants, USA
    George Nelson & Company, USA, date unknown
    An elegantly illustrated globe reflects the name
    and international clientele of an exclusive bar
    and restaurant.
9. **International Marketing** property, USA
    The Brothers Bogusky, USA, 1972
    A double globe illustrates the international scope
    of this property brand.
10. **Action Now Network** charity, USA
    Siah Design, USA, 2008
    Hands reach out around the world in this
    symbol for an organization that connects
    people with charities.

1.

2.

3.

4.

5.

6.

7.

8.

9.

10.

11.

12.

13.

14.

1. **Parents and Children** education, Switzerland
    Niklaus Troxler, Switzerland, 1998
    Organization promoting contact between parents
    and children, teachers and pupils.
2. **Fairtrade** quality certification, international
    Interbrand, international, 2002
    A globally consistent and recognizable symbol
    for an organization seeking to promote fair prices
    for producers in developing countries.
3. **Palatinose** food and beverages, Japan
    Bravis International Limited, Japan, 2002
    Recalling the silhouette of a child, this symbol for
    a Mitsui Sugar Company Limited sub-brand was
    designed to look natural, gentle and reassuring.
4. **Bitec Gewürzmüller GmbH** biotechnology,
    Germany
    Büro Uebele Visuelle Kommunikation, Germany, 1990
    A chromosome in the metaphase symbolizes the
    company's field of activity.
5. **Cingular Wireless** telecoms, USA
    VSA Partners, Inc., USA, 2000
    Symbol supporting the brand's positioning as a
    refreshing alternative in the wireless industry,
    focused on technology as an enabler of human
    communications. Cingular Wireless is a division
    of AT&T Inc., formerly SBC Communications.

6. **Finnish Refugee Council** non-governmental
    organizations, Finland
    Porkka & Kuutsa, Finland, 2008
    A simple symbol that transcends language
    barriers for a UNHCR (The UN Refugee Agency)
    partner providing information, support, training
    and social work for refugees and returnees.
7. **Yota** telecoms, Russia
    300Million, UK, 2008
    A playful and distinctive symbol for the world's
    first commercially available 4G mobile service.
8. **Dexmo** education, UK
    38one, USA, 2006
    Online resource where students can share
    knowledge and help each other to study
    and revise.
9. **Kunstuitleen Utrecht** libraries,
    The Netherlands
    Anker & Strijbos, The Netherlands, 2006
    Expressing notions of unified diversity, this
    warm symbol, which takes on both human
    and bibliophilic forms, is a treated extract from a
    comprehensive identity system designed for the
    provincial art library of Utrecht, comprising seven
    municipal art libraries.

10. **Hospital for Special Surgery** healthcare, USA
    Arnold Saks Associates, USA, 1995
    An animated figure expresses health and vitality.
11. **Institute for Citizenship** charity, UK
    Atelier Works, UK, 1995
    An organization whose aim is to engage young
    people with politics and civic life.
12. **Safety Consultant** government, Switzerland
    Adolf Flückiger, Switzerland, date unknown
    A protected human figure communicates the
    mission of a health-and-safety consultancy.
13. **Museo de Ciencia y Tecnología** arts and
    culture, Spain
    Cruz más Cruz, Spain, 1980
    A symbol of man's interaction with science (and
    perhaps a homage to Vitruvian man) for Spain's
    Museum of Science and Technology.
14. **Uroda** health and beauty, Poland
    Karol Sliwka, Poland, 1967
    A stylized figure provides a cosmetics brand
    with a bold, modern image.

15.

16.

15. Minnesota Dental Association healthcare, USA
Franke + Fiorella, USA, 2006
A warm, celebratory mark for a membership
organization protecting dental health.

16. Liceum Stenotypi education, Poland
Karol Sliwka, Poland, 1994
Symbol expressing the notion of collective
learning.

17. Toyota Housing Corporation property
development, Japan
Bravis International Limited, Japan, 2003
Symbol representing a family unit whose life has
been enriched by its Toyota home.

18. Family Communications broadcasting, USA
Essex Two, USA, 1983
A simple, warm image of a typical family unit
for an educational broadcaster and publisher.

19. Born Learning Chicago education, USA
Essex Two, USA, 2006
Symbol commissioned by Civitas for an
initiative providing early educational opportunities
for children.

20. March of Dimes charity, USA
Pentagram, USA, 1998
This mark reflects a broader mission for a charity
established in 1930 to fight polio: ensuring a
healthy start for all babies.

21. Freshfields Bruckhaus Deringer LLP
legal, UK
Gottschalk + Ash International, Switzerland, 2000
A stylized angel for an international law firm
expresses notions of moral certitude.

22. Maishima Sports Island sport and leisure, Japan
Ken Miki & Associates, Japan, 1994
An elegant, non-gender-specific figure suggests
motion and energy in this symbol for a public
sports facility.

17.

18.

19

20.

21.

22.

23.

24.

25.

26.

27.

28.

29.

30.

31.

32

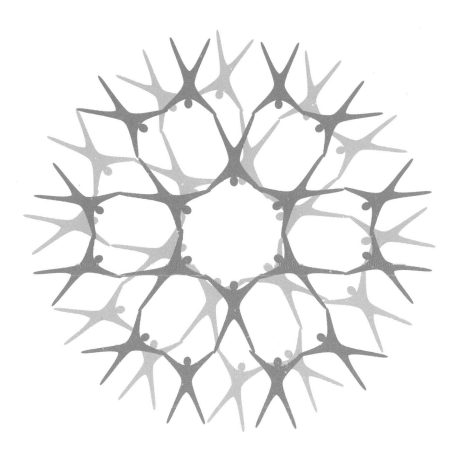

23. Da Vinci Physiomed healthcare, Germany
Q2 Design, Austria, 2005
Energetic mark reflecting the physiotherapy
and rehabilitation on offer at this Berlin clinic.

24. Ratcliffe Stott Architects architecture, UK
NB: Studio, UK, 2004
Two silhouettes recall the scale-figures used in
architectural drawings; both elements are in step
with each other, indicating that the practice has
one foot in architecture and one in interior design.

25. The Children's Fund charity, UK
Minale Tattersfield, UK, 1999
A cheerful paper chain conveys the central role of
children and the need to listen to their voices and
aspirations in this symbol for an organization
charged with helping economically disadvantaged
families with young children.

26. Toi Com Moi retail, France
FL@33, UK, 2003
A playful symbol for an independent Paris-based
clothing label aimed at the whole family; fathers
and sons, and mothers and daughters can find
identical items.

27. Thoresens Kulturformidling
arts and culture, Norway
Steiner Graphics, Canada, 2004
Three figures on a musical stave communicate
warmth and movement for a company
representing dancers, musicians and
performance artists.

28. Johnnie Walker beverages, USA
Identica, UK, 1997
This refreshed symbol is part of a broader
branding programme aimed at a more
cosmopolitan market.

29. 13th Maccabiah Sports Event sport and
leisure/events, Israel
Dan Reisinger, Israel, 1986
A dynamic symbol suggests the heat of
competition. Designed for the Maccabi Jewish
sports organization.

30. Jeeves dry-cleaning, UK
HGV, UK, 2005
Symbol for a leading UK dry-cleaners. Both
the imagery and the style evoke the era of
P. G. Wodehouse's Jeeves.

31. Royal Tropical Institute arts and culture,
The Netherlands
Edenspiekermann, The Netherlands, 2006
A 'tree of life' symbol represents nature,
knowledge, expertise and international,
intercultural cooperation.

32. Interuniversitaire Samenwerking
healthcare, Belgium
Chilli Design & Multimedia, Belgium, 2009
A circle made strong through human
collaboration is a visual metaphor for an
inter-university dentistry initiative focused
on training and peer reviews.

1.

2.

3.

4.

5.

6.

7.

8.

1. **Totes Kids** clothing and accessories, USA
   Automatic Art and Design, USA, 1998
   Playful mark for the children's line from umbrella brand Totes: the brand's iconic symbol is turned upside down and an eye is added.

2. **Innocent Drinks** food and beverages, UK
   Deepend, UK, 1999
   A naive, hand-drawn saint represents a popular brand of natural fruit smoothies, juices and vegetable pots.

3. **The Mind Trust** education, USA
   Lodge Design, USA, 2006
   A playful interpretation of turning cogs, this symbol is for an organization seeking to improve the lives of children in public schools.

4. **Scarecrow Wine** food and beverages, USA
   Vanderbyl Design, USA, 2006
   A stylized scarecrow indicates the name and wholesome personality of this Californian wine brand.

5. **Polski Zwiazek Zwyklych Kobiet**
   religion, Poland
   Karol Sliwka, Poland, 1991
   A warm, approachable mark for a women's religious organization.

6. **Saxenburgh Groep** healthcare, The Netherlands
   Studio Bau Winkel, The Netherlands, 2002
   An affable face represents a group with hospitals, clinics and care centres in the Dutch towns of Hardenburg and Coevorden.

7. **Indian Head** conglomerates, USA
   Chermayeff & Geismar, USA, 1971
   A proud American motif for a diversified conglomerate with myriad companies and interests.

8. **Windquest Racing Yacht** sport and leisure, USA
   Vanderbyl Design, USA, 2006
   The silhouetted profile and winged helmet recall the Greek god Mercury while expressing the idea of travel.

9.

10.

11.

12.

9. **Kokusai Syoken** finance, Japan
Katsuichi Ito Design Office, Japan, 1983
This symbol for a stockbroker expresses
vigilance, intelligence and integrity.

10. **PBS (Public Broadcasting Service)**
broadcasting, USA
Chermayeff & Geismar, USA, 1984
Repeated three times, this stylized profile of a
human face playfully puts the 'public' in public
television.

11. **Brainshell** patenting, Germany
Thomas Manss & Company, Germany, 2002
Brainshell looks at intellectual property from the
university's perspective as well as commercially,
an approach illustrated by these six heads in
alternating colours.

12. **Pro Golf IQ** sport and leisure, Australia
Magpie Studio, UK, 2008
Symbol combining golf and the mind for a
programme aimed at helping golfers to improve
their game.

13. **Princess Cruises** transport/travel, USA
Ken Parkhurst, USA, 1965
This evocative mark was known as the 'Love
Boat' symbol, thanks to a popular TV series based
on cruise ships.

14. **Academy of Achievement** non-profit
organizations, USA
Pentagram, USA, 1991
Non-profit foundation connecting young people
with America's achievers.

15. **BAFTA (British Academy of Film and
Television Arts)** entertainment, UK
Rose, UK, 2007
An evolution of BAFTA's bronze mask symbol,
originally designed in 1955.

16. **Mutual of Omaha** insurance, USA
Crosby Associates, USA, 2001
A modern reinterpretation of the iconic symbol
representing an Omaha chief helped to revitalize
this home, life, property and casualty insurance
company.

17. **Chartered Society of Designers** professional
associations, UK
Webb & Webb Design, UK, 1981
Minerva – Greek goddess of poetry, wisdom and
crafts – provided creative inspiration for the CSD's
mark. Originally designed for the CSD Medal, the
symbol has led the society's identity since 2003.

18. **Bentham Association** education, UK
Rose, UK, 2008
A stylized portrait of the 18th-century legal and
social reformer Jeremy Bentham symbolizes the
UCL (University College London) Law Faculty's
Alumni group.

13.

14.

15.

16

17.

18.

CBS (Columbia Broadcasting System)

Broadcasting, USA
William Golden, USA, 1951

Drive through Pennsylvania Dutch country today and you may still come across the Shaker barns that inspired William Golden (1911–59) to design one of the most celebrated and recognizable symbols in the history of graphic design. Frank Stanton, president of CBS at a time when television was becoming more popular than radio, wanted to establish a distinct identity for the network that would reflect its role as an innovative trailblazer. Stanton approached Golden who, in his role as creative director of CBS-TV's Advertising and Sales Promotion Department, worked with a talented team of designers – including the legendary Lou Dorfsman (1918–2008). The result was the famous 'all-seeing eye', which premiered on Saturday 20 October 1951.

Golden originally conceived the eye as 'a symbol in motion (consisting) of several concentric eyes – the camera dollies in to reveal the "pupil" as an iris diaphragm shutter which clicked open to show the station identification and clicked shut'. In a video on the history of the design (see YouTube) Lou Dorfsman cites Shaker barns as the main inspiration for the logo: many of them are adorned with symbols designed to ward off evil spirits, often in the form of an all-seeing eye. Dorfsman also recalls Golden's concern over what he should do as an encore as he had initially regarded the eye as part of a campaign, rather than a permanent identity. He need not have worried: although the symbol has been used in different colours and sizes over the years, CBS has never tampered with the original, which remains an exceptional and timeless design.

William Golden, 1955.

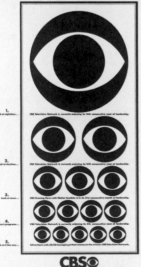

iNNoVaTe!

When a network program schedule keeps winning the largest nationwide audiences for six years, the natural instinct is to leave well enough alone. But the trick is not only to give fresh twists to old favorites but to break out with exciting new programs. You do it with a unique courtroom series dramatizing the terrifying moral choices of the law (like "The Defenders" whose premiere outrated the other two networks combined!)...or with programs that satisfy the city dweller's yearning for the simple life (like "Ichabod and Me" and "Window on Main Street")...or with captivating fantasies of talking horses and singing chipmunks...You add the element of adventure to the comedy of Bob Cummings, or create a team of smooth investigators who track down their quarry with style...You refresh the air with the comic spirit of Dick Van Dyke, the hilarity of a best-seller ("Father of the Bride"), the adventures of a pioneer circus, the heart-warming humor of a "Molly" Berg as a college freshman ...This kind of innovation carries the rich promise that in the intense competition for viewers, the CBS Television Network and its advertisers will once again **dominaTe**

  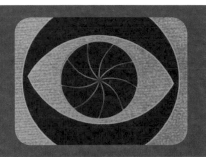

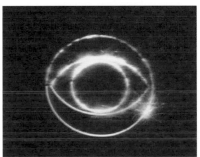  

1.

2.

3.

4.

5.

6.

7.

8.

9.

10.

11.

12.

13.

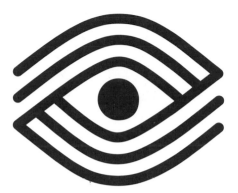

14.

1. **Handelsschule** education, Germany
Ernst Jupp, Germany, date unknown
Symbol for a business school.

2. **Vivid** media, UK
Clusta, UK, 2004
Modified version of an existing symbol for a hire company specializing in film and digital video equipment.

3. **Allergan Pharmaceuticals** pharmaceuticals, USA
Denis and Ken Parkhurst, USA, 1970
Symbol for a consumer eye-care brand.

4. **Jeune France** politics, France
Look, France, 1972
A stylized eye expresses the vigilant, progressive outlook of a political association for young people.

5. **Office of the Human Rights Ombudsman**
representative bodies, Slovenia
Armada d.o.o., Slovenia, 2002
Mark symbolizing the body responsible for monitoring and protecting human rights in Slovenia.

6. **Cloud Shield** information technology, USA
Pentagram, USA, 2001
A suitably sentient mark for a computer network security company.

7. **Naigai Technos** construction, Japan
Katsuichi Ito Design Office, Japan, 1993
A combination of two simple shapes communicates the work of a company specializing in elements such as partition walls, glass sliding walls and flooring for interior construction.

8. **Sign Design Society** professional associations, UK
Atelier Works, UK, 1992
An association of clients, designers and manufacturers involved in developing signs and sign systems.

9. **Pinkerton's, Inc.** security, USA
BrandEquity, USA, 1983–84
A modern adaptation of the eye symbol used by Pinkerton's since the 1850s.

10. **Städtli Optik** healthcare, Switzerland
Erich Brechbühl (Mixer), Switzerland, 2004
A stylized eye communicates the client's area of business: optometry.

11. **Moskau GmbH** arts and culture, Austria
Moniteurs GmbH, Germany, 2008
An elegant mark hints at the heritage of the renovated Café Moskau in Berlin.

12. **Center for Industrial Design** arts and culture, Bulgaria
Stefan Kanchev, Bulgaria, c.1960s–70s
Symbol suggesting both aesthetics and the practical applications of industrial design.

13. **Conservation Trust of Puerto Rico** non-profit organizations, USA/Puerto Rico
Chermayeff & Geismar, USA, 1979
A vigilant symbol for a private, non-profit entity that owns and manages environmentally sensitive properties in Puerto Rico.

14. **Time Warner** broadcasting/media, USA
Chermayeff & Geismar, USA, 1989
When Time Inc. and Warner Brothers merged in 1989, Time Warner chairman Steve Ross was keen to place equal emphasis on both companies. The resulting symbol, designed by C&G's Steff Geissbuhler and launched in 1989, achieved just that. With a spiral emerging from the pupil, this simply drawn eye turns into an ear, deftly encompassing the scope of Time Warner's media empire. Today, the symbol is used by Time Warner Cable, part of Time Warner until 2009 when it was 'spun out' to shareholders.

15.

16.

17.

18.

15. Genesee Health Systems healthcare, USA
R. Roger Remington, USA, 1969
A distinctive mark recalls the form of a human eye, echoing vigilance and, perhaps, elements of the company name.

16. Biennial Exhibition of Trademarks events, Bulgaria
Stefan Kanchev, Bulgaria, c.1960s–70s
Symbol suggesting the act of seeing that was designed for an exhibition of symbols.

17. Mazetti food and beverages, Sweden
Olle Eksell, Sweden, 1956
Eksell's iconic eyes, winner of an international competition to find a new look for a confectionery brand, establish a memorable visual language.

18. Melos Inc. transport, Japan
Ken Miki & Associates, Japan, 1990
A series of simplified eye-shapes also suggest boats, the mode of transport offered by this Japanese company.

19. Pro Radio-Television broadcasting, Switzerland
Werner Mühlemann , Switzerland, date unknown
Both sound and vision are illustrated in this simple yet clever symbol.

20. Société Industrielle de Lunetterie manufacturing, France
Publicité Pezet, France, 1969
A stylized eye suggests precision as well as the optical products manufactured by the client.

21. Hydrotech Corp exploration, USA
The Brothers Bogusky, USA, 1967
Symbol suggesting the interaction between humans, technology and water.

22. Medicornea healthcare, USA
Denis and Ken Parkhurst, USA, 1985
Symbol for a Seattle, Washington, manufacturer of precision intracorneal lenses used to correct cataracts.

23. CEDFI film, France
Niklaus Troxler, Switzerland, 1973
Eyes and camera lenses provided the inspiration for this symbol for a producer of commercial films.

24. Future Focus public services, UK
Graphical House, UK, 2008
A stylized eye motif suggests both the broadcaster and the viewer in this symbol for an audience development initiative.

19.

20.

21.

22.

23.

24.

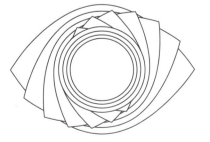

1.

2.

3.

4.

5.

6.

7.

8.

9.

10.

11.

12.

13.

1. **Footprint Handbooks** publishing, UK
   Mytton Williams Ltd, UK, 1999
   A simple footprint suggests exploration and
   adventure in this symbol for a publisher of
   travel guides.
2. **WEC** consultancies/environmental advocacy,
   Australia
   North Design & Branding, Australia, 2008
   A footprint with topographic lines is the symbol
   for a consultancy firm focused on environmental
   sustainability.
3. **Shuropody** healthcare, UK
   The One Off, UK, 2007
   A healthy footprint supports the natural
   treatments promoted by the UK's leading
   footcare retailer.
4. **Chicago Children's Hospital** healthcare, USA
   Essex Two, USA, 2000
   A child's hand provides this Chicago hospital
   with a striking graphic image.
5. **Freedom Healthcare** healthcare, USA
   Essex Two, USA, 1990
   Symbol conveying a hands-on approach to
   in-home healthcare.

6. **One Blue Sphere** Internet, UK
   Magpie Studio, UK, 2008
   This symbol for an international online scuba
   diving resource adopts the universal sign
   language used by divers.
7. **Okanagan Spring** beverages, Canada
   Subplot Design Inc., Canada, 2008
   A barley sheaf in an open hand symbolizes
   a passionate hands-on approach, and the
   ingredients employed by British Columbia's
   leading craft beer brand.
8. **Helen Brown Massage Therapist**
   health and beauty, UK
   Magpie Studio, UK, 2008
   Tools of the trade, these hands also hint
   at the business owner's name.
9. **Intergracja Gospodarcza** economic aid, Poland
   Karol Sliwka, Poland, 1973
   Symbol for Rada Wzajemnej Pomocy
   Gospodarczej, the council for mutual
   economic aid.

10. **Handball Weltmeisterschaft** sport and
    leisure, Germany
    Stankowski + Duschek, Germany, 1982
    A simple hand and ball motif for the Handball
    World Championship.
11. **Ten Fingers Folk Art Gallery** arts and culture,
    Israel
    Dan Reisinger, Israel, 1974
    An illustrative symbol suggests the art gallery's
    name and the handmade qualities of the exhibits.
12. **B2B Equality** technology, USA
    Pentagram, USA, 2000
    Mark symbolizing electronic information exchange
    for start-up companies and entrepreneurs.
13. **The Waterways Trust** environmental
    advocacy, UK
    Pentagram, UK, 2000
    Agency promoting the conservation and
    regeneration of Britain's inland waterways.

14.

15.

16.

17.

18.

14. Amnesty 30 Years charity/events, Finland
Hahmo, Finland, 1996
A celebratory symbol featuring six hands –
a finger for each of 30 years.

15. Caspian Energy community initiatives,
Azerbaijan
Carter Wong Design, UK, 2004
Symbol for an initiative educating children about
energy; their handprints illustrate the ultimate
energy source – the sun.

**16. ASSH (American Society for Surgery of the
Hand)** healthcare, USA
9MYLES, Inc., USA, 2007–08
A dynamic mark expresses the idea of unified
strength as well as the society's specialist area.

17. Escuela Superior de Relaciones Públicas
education, Spain
El Paso, Galería de Comunicación, Spain, 2005
A circle of touching hands conveys
communication for a public-relations school.

18. HandsOn Network non-profit organizations, USA
Duffy & Partners, USA, 2008
Effervescent symbol for a network that inspires,
equips and mobilizes people to take action that
changes the world.

1.

2.

3.

4.

5.

6.

7.

8.

9.

1. **Badisches Landesmuseum Karlsruhe**
   arts and culture, Germany
   Stankowski + Duschek, Germany, 1992
   Symbol echoing the shape of the famous
   Karlsruhe Palace.
2. **John Hoole Estate Agents** property, UK
   Hold, UK, 2006
   A modern, residential idyll representing a
   Brighton-based estate agent.
3. **Approved Construction: Tam O'Shanter
   Glen** property development, Canada
   Raymond Lee, Canada, 1970
   Symbol suggesting the integrity and quality of
   a housing development in Thornhill, Ontario.

4. **Fasaddoktorn** construction, Sweden
   Q2 Design, Austria, 2003
   A house bearing a familiar first-aid cross is the
   symbol for what translates as a 'facade doctor'.
5. **Coram** charity, UK
   Pentagram, UK, 1999
   This symbol is part of a warm, hopeful identity for
   the UK's oldest children's charity.
6. **Housale** property development, Greece
   Chris Trivizas, Greece, 2008
   The mark suggests integrity; the stylized house
   and ladder motifs refer to the company's services.

7. **Budmax** construction, Poland
   Logotypy.com, Poland, 2004
   The familiar form of a residential building conveys
   the nature of the client's business with clarity.
8. **Sanwa Sogo Building Co., Ltd.**
   construction, Japan
   Yoshioka Design Room, Japan, 1965
   The familiar outline of a house for a Tokyo
   building firm.
9. **Boagaz** plumbing, Switzerland
   Hi, Switzerland, 2007
   This symbol is part of an identity designed for a
   new, easy-to-install gas system developed by Boa
   AG Rothenburg.

10.

11.

12.

13.

14.

15.

10. Sheffield Cathedral religion, UK
The Workshop, UK, 2008
Symbol conveying the cathedral's distinctive archway and its open-door ethos. A closer look reveals one person supporting another.

11. Daniel Tower Hotel hospitality, Israel
Dan Reisinger, Israel, 1972
Symbol referencing the hotel's architecture.

12. Preservation League of New York State non-profit organizations, USA
Chermayeff & Geismar, USA, 1974
Symbol for an organization dedicated to preserving New York State's historic buildings, districts and landscapes.

13. Scripps Howard media, USA
Chermayeff & Geismar, USA, 1984
A beacon of light shines out of the dark, conveying the illuminating mission of a diversified media company.

14. Rockefeller Center property development, USA
Chermayeff & Geismar, USA, 1985
This elegant mark recalls the soaring architecture and famous Art Deco style of this Manhattan landmark, as well as the concept of a centre within the city.

15. The Tower property development, USA
Design Has No Name (DHNN), Argentina, 2007
A simple graphic representation of a skyscraper for a development in New York.

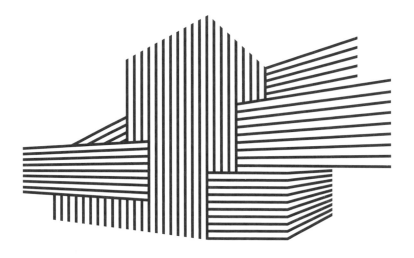

Nouveau Théâtre de Montreuil

Arts and culture, France
Aurélie Gasche & Delphine Cordier, France, 2007

Opened in 1989, the Centre Dramatique National, the Nouveau Théâtre's predecessor, provided Montreuil in northern France with a vibrant hub for the performing arts; its broad remit encompassed theatre, dance, music, visual arts and architecture. Portuguese architect Alvaro Siza's master plan for the urban regeneration of Montreuil has brought about a steady transformation and, perhaps due its location opposite the town hall, the Centre Dramatique National was earmarked for an architectural makeover. Rather than renovate the existing building, French architects Dominique Coulon et associés were appointed to design a new purpose-built theatre on the site of the old one. Nominated in 2009 for a prestigious Mies van der Rohe Award, Coulon's celebrated design has provided Montreuil's town centre with an architectural gem; perhaps that's why, rather than reverting to the old name, the theatre reopened in January 2009 as the Nouveau Théâtre de Montreuil.

As with Jean Widmer and the Pompidou (see pages 274–277), Coulon's signature building provided the ideal starting point for the theatre's identity. While Aurélie Gasche and Delpine Cordier developed a number of ideas for this – including several purely typographic routes – they settled on a three-dimensional image of the building. However, rather than simply echo the building's outline, Gasche and Cordier created a celebratory mark with lines bursting out from the building's core: an expression of the theatre's dynamic, creative and often innovative programme of events.

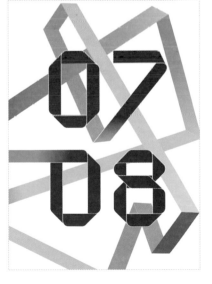

16.

17.

18.

19.

20.

21.

16. Swiss RE (30 St Mary Axe) property
development, UK
Attik, UK/USA, 2002
An elegant mark mirroring the curvilinear form of this
London landmark. Swiss Re (widely known as the
'gherkin') was designed by Foster + Partners.

17. Infrastructure Partnerships Australia
infrastructure, Australia
North Design & Branding, Australia, 2008
Roads and buildings are combined in this symbol for
Australia's peak infrastructure forum, which focuses
on public policy interests.

18. Fundacja Wspólpracy Polsko Niemieckiej
international relations, Poland
Karol Sliwka, Poland, 1992
A stylized bridge symbolizes the organization's
attempts to connect different nations and cultures.

19. Wembley Stadium sport and leisure, UK
Identica, UK, 2004
An elegant impression of the stadium and its
landmark arch – a fitting icon for 'the home of
football'.

20. House of Switzerland sport and leisure,
Switzerland
Büro Destruct, Switzerland, 2003
This symbol is part of an identity designed for
the Swiss presence at the 2004 Olympic Games
in Athens.

21. Slagelse Kommune municipality, Denmark
Bysted, Denmark, 2006
Mark for a municipality in eastern Denmark;
one of several designed by Bysted following
a programme of municipal reform.

22.

23.

24.

25.

26.

27.

22. Nizhegorodskaya Lift manufacturing, Russia
Peter-Designer Studio, Russia, 2004
This symbol communicates the nature of the
lift business with a simple perspective view of
the top of a building.

23. Conflict retail, The Netherlands
Boy Bastiaens, The Netherlands, 2005
The mark for a furniture store juxtaposes a
castle – symbolizing tradition and residence –
with dark clouds for a visual conflict.

24. Conarc Modular Building Systems
construction, USA
Primo Angeli Graphics, USA, 1970
A repeated architectural motif indicates the
modular building systems developed by Conarc.

25. International Congress of Immunology
events, Italy
KMstudio, Italy, 2008
Monumental architectural symbol for a congress
organized by leading Italian events brand Gruppo
Triumph.

26. BWA arts and culture, Czech Republic
Karol Sliwka, Poland, 1978–79
Symbol for the Biuro Wystaw Artystycznych
(artistic exhibitions office).

27. Gotham Books publishing, USA
The O Group, USA, 2002
A mythic, 'open-book' skyscraper references the
New York home of this Penguin imprint (Gotham is
a nickname for New York City).

28.

29.

30.

31.

32.

28. Congreso de la Unión Internacional de Arquitectos events, Spain
Cruz más Cruz, Spain, 1974
A bold architectural image designed to promote a congress of the International Union of Architects.

29. Rose Theatre arts and culture, UK
NB: Studio, UK, 2001
The Rose, Bankside's first theatre, was built in 1587 and excavated in 1989; the symbol shows the new rose blossoming from the old London theatre.

30. Hochschule Luzern - Soziale Arbeit social work, Switzerland
Hi, Switzerland, 2006
Symbol evoking the theme of global communities. It was designed for Lucerne University of Applied Sciences and Arts.

31. The Cape hospitality, Australia
Design By Pidgeon, Australia, 2004
Part of a major renaming and branding exercise, this new symbol is inspired by the landmark lighthouse at the Cape Schanck Resort on Australia's Mornington Peninsula.

32. Akademie der Bildenden Künste München education, Germany
BÜRO ALBA, Germany, 2008
Symbol presenting an altogether contemporary take on the academy's historic building.

33.

34.

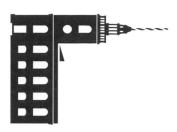

35.

36.

37.

38.

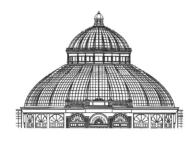

33. Big Ben 150th Anniversary government, UK
Hyperkit, UK, 2009
Symbol celebrating the birthday of London's most iconic bell and clock tower (copyright Palace of Westminster).

34. St. Mary's Church, Rotherhithe religion, UK
Rose, UK, 2009
An upended church becomes a drill in this symbol designed to promote fundraising for a major restoration project.

35. Matchworks property development, UK
Uniform, UK, 2006
Symbol echoing the central architectural feature of a commercial regeneration development in Liverpool led by Urban Splash.

36. Jamaica Station transport, USA
Pentagram, USA, 1998
Symbol recalling the large curved roof and tracks of the New York railway station – the major hub and headquarters of the Long Island Rail Road.

37. Ruskin Square urban development, UK
Figtree, UK, 2007
An architectural symbol for a landmark development encompassing homes, commercial spaces, retail opportunities and cultural venues.

38. New York Botanical Garden arts and culture, USA
Pentagram, USA, 2000
Symbol inspired by the famous Enid A. Haupt conservatory building at one of the world's oldest and largest botanical gardens.

Centre Georges Pompidou

Arts and culture, France
Jean Widmer, Switzerland, 1977

One of the French capital's finest cultural attractions and one of its most striking architectural landmarks, the Centre Georges Pompidou was the brainchild of French President Georges Pompidou (1911–74), whose ambition to create an original cultural institution in Paris was fulfilled by this groundbreaking endeavour. Known locally as Beaubourg because of its location in the city's 4th arrondissement, the Pompidou Centre focuses on modern and contemporary creativity, encompassing the visual arts, design, architecture, theatre, music and cinema.

Construction of the centre's idiosyncratic home, designed by Renzo Piano and Richard Rogers, began in 1971 but wasn't completed until 1977, three years after Pompidou's death. Officially opened on 31 January 1977, the Pompidou offers a radical design – with its exposed structural and service elements – and a diverse programme of events and exhibitions that have proved a huge draw to visitors: around 9 million people pass through its doors every year, amounting to over 190 million visitors in just over 30 years.

The architectural treat served up by Piano and Rogers also provided the inspiration for Jean Widmer's symbol: a bold and distinctly modern interpretation of the building with six horizontal stripes intersected by the Pompidou's famous exterior stairway, zigzagging from left to right across the facade. It is an incredibly simple illustration of the building and yet, in capturing the creativity and dynamism of its exposed structure, Widmer expresses the values that led to the foundation of the Pompidou Centre and to its continuing success.

Christine Albanel
Ministre de la Culture et de la Communication

Alain Seban
Président du Centre Pompidou

Alfred Pacquement
Directeur du Musée national d'art moderne / Centre de création industrielle

vous prient de bien vouloir assister à l'inauguration de l'exposition

JACQUES VILLEGLÉ
LA COMÉDIE URBAINE
MARDI 16 SEPTEMBRE 2008
17H – 21H30
GALERIE 2, NIVEAU 6

Exposition présentée du 17 septembre 2008 au 5 janvier 2009
Invitation valable uniquement ce jour, pour deux personnes, sur présentation de ce carton
Fermeture à 22 heures

En partenariat média avec Métrobus et Métro

Jacques Villeglé : Rues Desprez et Vercingétorix - La Femme, 1966. Museum Ludwig, Cologne – Allemagne. © Adagp, Paris 2008
© Centre Pompidou, Direction de la communication - Conception graphique : Ch. Beneyton, 2008

PRESSE
11H-15H

**Centre
Pompidou**

ACCOMPAGNATEUR

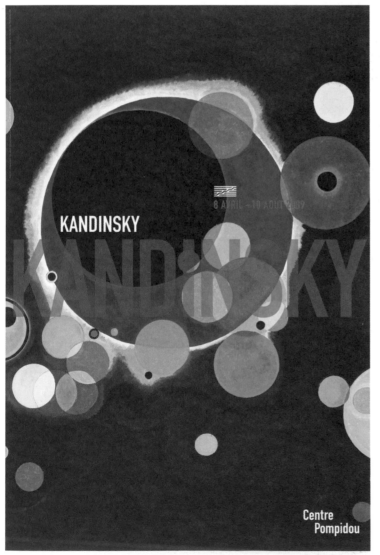

KANDINSKY

**Centre
Pompidou**

Christine Albanel
Ministre de la Culture et de la Communication

Alain Seban
Président du Centre Pompidou

Alfred Pacquement
Directeur du Musée national d'art moderne / Centre de création industrielle

vous prient de bien vouloir assister à l'inauguration de l'exposition

GAUDIER–BRZESKA
DANS LES COLLECTIONS
DU MUSÉE NATIONAL D'ART MODERNE
MARDI 23 JUIN 2009
18H – 21H30
MUSÉE, GALERIE D'ART GRAPHIQUE, NIVEAU 4

Exposition réalisée avec la participation du Musée des Beaux-Arts d'Orléans
présentée du 24 juin au 14 septembre 2009
Invitation valable uniquement ce jour, pour deux personnes, sur présentation de ce carton
Fermeture à 21 heures

Gaudier-Brzeska : «Femme assise», 1914, Don de la Kettle's Yard Foundation, 1966, MNAM. Adam Rzepka.
Coll. Centre Pompidou, MnamCci.
© Centre Pompidou, direction de la communication, conception graphique : Ch. Beneyton, 2009

**Centre
Pompidou**

**Centre
Pompidou** laissez-passer
www.centrepompidou.fr 01 44 78 14 63

CATALOGUE DES ÉDITIONS 2010

**Centre
Pompidou**

1.

2.

3.

4.

5.

6.

7.

8.

9.

10.

11.

12.

13.

1. **Kayak** Internet/tourism, USA
BrandEquity, USA, 2005
The symbol for an online travel resource depicts an aerial view of a kayak but also an eye, implying the Internet 'search'.

2. **Flight Series** sport and leisure, USA
Satellite Design, USA, 2002
A dynamic symbol echoing the name of a sub-brand belonging to The North Face.

3. **Delta Airlines** transport, USA
Lippincott, USA, 2007
The symbol respects the airline's heritage while announcing a fresh look prompted by Delta's desire to retain its position as an industry leader.

4. **Kou Nakamura** arts and culture, Japan
Good Design Company, Japan, 2006
Symbol for a Japanese novelist.

5. **Airport School** transport, Italy
KMstudio, Italy, 2008
A playful paper aeroplane communicates a warm, approachable spirit.

6. **YouSendIt** Internet, USA
Connie Hwang, USA, 2004
A paper aeroplane reflects the swift service offered by one of the Internet's leading digital-content delivery brands.

7. **Danish Air Transport** transport, Denmark
Finn Nygaard, Denmark, 1997
Based in Vamdrup, Denmark, DAT operates scheduled passenger and cargo services to various destinations.

8. **Unlimited Travel Group** travel, Sweden
Dolhem Design, Sweden, 2006
A circular motif with cropped aeroplane outlines provides a simple metaphor for 'unlimited' global travel.

9. **Airtrain** transport, USA
Pentagram, USA, 1998
New York City's first direct rail link to John F. Kennedy International Airport.

10. **Icon Aircraft** transport, USA
Attik, UK/USA, 2007
Symbol for a brand of aircraft designed to capitalize on new FAA regulations enabling non-pilots to earn their Light Sport Aircraft (LSA) licence in as little as two weeks.

11. **Newcruise Yacht Projects & Design** sport and leisure, Germany
Tilt Design Studio, Germany, 2008
A refined, aspirational sail motif for an internationally acclaimed company designing 'super' yachts.

12. **Motorcheck** insurance, UK
Rose, UK, 2005
A playful symbol softens the profile of a vehicle-checking service for insurance companies.

13. **AutoStore** automotive, UK
Rose, UK, 2006
Symbol for a mobile body-shop repair service that promises to make a damaged car 'as good as new in no time'.

14.

15.

16.

17.

18.

19.

20.

14. **Norsk Hydro** energy, Norway
Siegel+Gale, USA, 2003
A dynamic sail motif recalls a history of
exploration and discovery in this symbol for
a Fortune 500 oil and aluminium company.

15. **BicycleTutor.com** Internet, USA
Siah Design, USA, 2008
Playful symbol for a website where people can
learn more about bikes and how to repair them.

16. **Flagship Global Health** healthcare, USA
Method Inc., USA, 2007
An elegant symbol, recalling a furled leaf and a
ship's sail, for a service helping people find quality
healthcare.

17. **Vasco da Gama** restaurants, Portugal
Bürocratik, Portugal, 2006
A stylized caravel pays homage to the
restaurant's namesake – one of Portugal's most
famous explorers.

18. **Rygaards School** education, Denmark
Punktum Design, Denmark, 2003
Symbol for an international school in Copenhagen.

19. **Maritime Museum of Victoria** arts and
culture, Australia
David Lancashire Design, Australia, 2002
An appropriately nautical endorsement awarded
by the government of Victoria to maritime areas of
interest or historical significance.

20. **New Bedford Whaling Museum** arts and
culture, USA
Malcolm Grear Designers, USA, 2000
A striking mark evoking the rich heritage of the
American whaling industry.

1.

2.

3.

1. **Martin Newcombe** property, UK
   Buddy, UK, 2008
   A spanner symbolizes maintenance, while its
   negative space suggests the shape of a house.
2. **Evangelize** media/religion, USA
   Siah Design, USA, 2008
   Religious iconography, the fish, meets technology
   in this symbol for a Christian website providing a
   range of media including sermons, illustrations,
   video clips and films.
3. **One Laptop Per Child** education, USA
   Pentagram, USA, 2006
   Stylized pictograms provide a literal translation of
   OLPC's aim to provide the world's poorest
   children with $100 computers.

4. **Videns** media, Argentina
   Bernardo + Celis, Argentina, 2004
   A simplified symbol suggesting both a watchful
   eye and a camera.
5. **UK Music Week** broadcasting, UK
   Together Design Ltd, UK, 2005
   Symbol for a radio initiative promoting British
   music and working in alliance with a range of
   stations. The symbol was part of an identity that
   had to appeal to different audiences and sit
   comfortably with other brands.
6. **Creative Zionism Association** business
   support, Israel
   Dan Reisinger, Israel, 1982
   Industrial cogs combine with a familiar symbol
   of Jewish culture in this mark for an organization
   supporting start-up industries.

7. **Cue32** advertising, South Africa
   Reghardt, South Africa, 2008
   Cogs convey industry and ingenuity for an
   advertising agency specializing in online and
   interactive media.
8. **IPCT** sport and leisure, Switzerland
   Erich Brechbühl (Mixer), Switzerland, 2006
   Bicycle chain links form the symbol for a union
   providing support to the leading teams in cycling.
9. **Gears Bike Shop** sport and leisure/retail, Canada
   Faith, Canada, 2008
   A simple graphic interpretation of the client's name.

4.

5.

6.

7.

8.

9.

1.

2.

3.

4.

5.

6.

7.

8.

1. **3D Retail** Internet/retail/information
    technology, USA
    Pentagram, USA, 2000
    A developer of immersive, 3-D Internet shopping
    applications for retailers.
2. **Meiji Yasuda Life Insurance
    Company** insurance, Japan
    Bravis International Limited, Japan, 2003
    Symbol based on a cradle in response to
    the client's desire to promote a kind and
    compassionate image.
3. **Matelsom** retail, France
    FL@33, UK, 2002
    The simplest geometric forms combine in an
    elegant symbol for France's leading online bed
    and mattress retailer.

4. **DFS** retail, UK
    FOUR IV, UK, 2005
    Dreaming of chairs; a simple and emotive symbol
    bridges the gap between product and consumer.
5. **Southern Poverty Law Center** legal, USA
    Chermayeff & Geismar, USA, 2008
    Simplified scales of justice provide the ideal
    mark for a non-profit legal organization in
    Montgomery, Alabama.
6. **Putnam Investments** finance, USA
    Carbone Smolan Agency, USA, 1991
    The weighing scales infer the strength and
    equilibrium of this investment corporation.
    Putnam's identity has since been refreshed,
    but the scales remain.

7. **Cliffhanger** retail, UK
    Magpie Studio, UK, 2007
    Ideogram suggesting both clothing and mountains
    for an independent retailer specializing in outdoor
    apparel.
8. **Wardrobe Therapy** consultancy/fashion, USA
    The O Group, USA, 2009
    A simple wire-frame coathanger with a first-aid
    cross completes the symbol for a fashion
    consultancy company.

9.

9. **Bulletin of the Atomic Scientist** non-profit
    organizations, USA
    Pentagram, USA, 2007
    Established in 1945, this organization is dedicated
    to security, science and survival in a nuclear world.

10. **Fireside** publishing, USA
    Pentagram, USA, 1999
    The mark for a Simon & Schuster imprint
    publishing games and self-improvement titles
    recalls the hearth.

11. **Filmaps** entertainment, Spain
    Siah Design, USA, 2009
    A cinematic map-pin for an online hub sharing
    information about film locations.

12. **Endeva** logistics, UK
    Carter Wong Design, UK, 2002
    A visual play on a three-pronged plug. Endeva
    distributes and services electrical goods for
    consumers and businesses.

13. **Film Center** arts and culture, Greece
    Chris Trivizas, Greece, 2008
    Rows of seats provide a simple and effective
    reference to cinematic culture.

10.

11.

12.

13.

14.

15.

16.

17.

14. Orange Pekoe food and beverages, UK
Together Design Ltd, UK, 2006
Symbol for a brand aiming to become an industry
leader in premium quality tea, offering a broad
selection of teas and upmarket tea rooms.

15. Clerys retail, Ireland
Creative Inc., Ireland, 2004
An aspirational mark recalls the heritage and
architecture of a popular department store
in Dublin.

16. Hornsby Interiors retail, UK
Mind Design, UK, 2007
A modified version of a traditional logo for an
antique dealer in London.

17. Atlas & Co. publishing, USA
The O Group, USA, 2005
A sextant conveys notions of exploration and
discovery in this symbol for an independent
publisher of quality non-fiction.

18. Mandarin Oriental hospitality, Hong Kong
Pentagram, UK, 1985
A stylized fan draws on the oriental heritage of
this leading international group of luxury hotels
and resorts.

18.

1.

2.

3.

4.

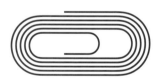

5.

6.

7.

8.

9.

10.

11.

12.

13.

1. **Golf Resorts International** sport and leisure, Australia
   Cato Partners, Australia, 1991
   A ball, the green and the cup are the ideal images to identify a leading golf-course developer.
2. **Basketball Europameisterschaften** sport and leisure, Germany
   Stankowski + Duschek, Germany, 1985
   A simple geometric illustration for the biennial European Basketball Championships.
3. **ICC (International Cricket Council)** sport and leisure, international
   Minale Tattersfield, UK, 2000
   A symbol that embraces a new spirit of international corporate accountability and ambition while returning to the roots and values at the heart of cricket.
4. **Tennis Club** sport and leisure, USA
   Benson Crane, USA, 1971
   The distinctive tennis-ball motif clearly conveys the focus of this sports club.

5. **Sports Centre Willlsau** sport and leisure, France
   Niklaus Troxler, Switzerland, 1997
   Symbol suggesting the wide range of activities on offer at a sports centre with several gymnasiums and a pool.
6. **Skischule Alpendorf** sport and leisure, Austria
   Modelhart Design, Austria, 2003
   An abstract winter sportsman represents freedom, fun and movement in this symbol for an Alpine ski school.
7. **Office Games** charity, UK
   The Partners, UK, 2009
   A playful mark combines a paper clip and athletics track to promote a spoof Olympics, where fun games such as 'floppy discus' and 'Post-it note relay races' raised funds for Richard House Children's Hospice.
8. **Golf La Moraleja** sport and leisure, Spain
   Cruz más Cruz, Spain, 1974
   Simple yet effective: a golf ball sits on a green, with the stripes in the background suggesting blue skies.
9. **Express Post** postal services, Australia
   Cato Partners, Australia, 1988
   Visual references to speed and the accuracy of archery symbolize Australia's overnight postal service.

10. **Premier Rugby** sport and leisure, UK
    Glazer, UK, 2000
    Symbol suggesting the strength, fluidity and speed of rugby union at its best.
11. **NBA (National Basketball Association)** sport and leisure, USA
    Siegel+Gale, USA, 1969
    Iconic symbol for one of America's leading professional sports associations.
12. **World Cup 94** sport and leisure, USA
    Pentagram, USA, 1993
    A soaring football and billowing American flag create a dynamic symbol for the 1994 World Cup.
13. **World Grand Champions Cup** sport and leisure, Japan
    Katsuichi Ito Design Office, Japan, 1994
    Stylized hands combine to express the coming together of different cultures for a volleyball tournament.

1.

2.

3.

4.

5.

6.

1. Morton & Peplow food and beverages, Germany
Magpie Studio, UK, 2007
Two symbols of Britishness – a bowler hat and a domed, silver-service platter – are combined for a Munich delicatessen specializing in British cuisine.

2. Footstep Films film, UK
Purpose, UK, 2004
A clapperboard becomes a suitcase in a symbol for a film-production company specializing in DVD travel guides.

3. Jigsaw Pictures film, USA
Denis Parkhurst, USA, 1996
Symbol for Alex Gibney, an independent maker of feature films and documentaries who is based in Hollywood.

4. Maritza textiles, Bulgaria
Stefan Kanchev, Bulgaria, c.1960s–70s
A stylized bobbin for a textile factory.

5. Artists' Services talent agency, USA
Hughes design/communications, USA, 2007
Tools of the trade; symbol designed for an agency representing artists and stylists working in the entertainment industry.

6. Anne Schmul fashion, Germany
Pfadfinderei, Gemany, 1999
An hairstyle-based symbol for a Berlin fashion designer.

7.

8.

9.

10.

11.

12.

7. **Canadian Industrial Editors** professional associations, Canada
Leslie Smart, Canada, 1970
Four fountain pens cross nibs to communicate a united front for editors.

8. **Kazue Morinaga soprano recital** music, Japan
Ken Miki & Associates, Japan, 1995
A cacophony of elegant musical notes represents the talent of one of Japan's most famous sopranos.

9. **National Opera** arts and culture/music, Bulgaria
Stefan Kanchev, Bulgaria, c.1960s–70s
A distinctly musical motif.

10. **The Grammy Awards** music, USA
Bright Strategic Design/Denis Parkhurst, USA, 2008
Symbol for the Recording Academy and its many affiliates.

11. **École Normale de Musique de Paris**
education, France
FL@33, UK, 2002
A bass clef, looking in isolation like a listening ear, provides the perfect symbol for an acclaimed and historic private music college in Paris.

12. **Türkische Kunstmusik** music, Germany
Ott+Stein, Germany, 1989
A musical note is laid on its side to reveal the crescent moon and star of the Turkish flag.

1.

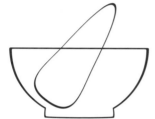

2.

3.

4.

5.

6.

1. **Hallwag Verlag** publishing, Germany
   KMS TEAM, Germany, 2002
   Symbol reflecting the focus of a *Graefe und Unzer*
   imprint devoted exclusively to literature about wine.
2. **The Prime Time** restaurants, USA
   Unimark International, USA, 1969
   Restaurant chain belonging to parent company
   Great Western.

3. **Nyonya** restaurants, UK
   FOUR IV, UK, 2005
   A pestle and mortar suggest the preparation of
   fresh ingredients, reflecting the quality of this
   Malaysian restaurant.
4. **Barnes Ltd** pharmaceuticals, UK
   Woudhuysen Design Group, UK, date unknown
   A pestle and mortar indicate the traditional
   process employed to mix pharmaceutical
   ingredients.

5. **MillerCoors** food and beverages, USA
   Pentagram, USA, 2008
   A simple aerial view of a glass is the symbol for
   a joint venture between brewing giants SABMiller
   and Molson Coors.
6. **Guild of Food Writers** professional
   associations, UK
   300Million, UK, 2006
   A witty and decidedly elegant symbol for a
   professional association of food writers and
   broadcasters.

7.

8.

9.

10.

11.

12.

7. **My Cuisine Canary Wharf** restaurants, UK
    Radford Wallis, UK, 2006
    A deceptively simple image for this restaurant:
    the negative space between the knife and fork
    creates the familiar outline of one of London's
    most iconic buildings.
8. **Erez Gordon Consultants** hospitality, Australia
    Anne Angel Designs, Australia, 2008
    A warm, approachable symbol for a company
    dealing in 'the business of food and wine'.

9. **Telmo Rodriguez** food and beverages, Spain
    Pentagram, UK, 2003
    Distinctive symbol for a winemaker who revives
    and re-creates Spanish wines that have slipped
    into obscurity.
10. **Caffè Tirreno** restaurants, Germany
    SWSP Design, Germany, 2005
    An appetizing mark for a Munich bar and café
    selling cocktails, light meals, coffee and, of
    course, cake.

11. **Planet Coffee** food and beverages, USA
    Automatic Art and Design, USA, 1997
    A simple, witty mark reflecting the name of a
    Columbus, Ohio, coffee shop.
12. **The Good Diner** restaurants, USA
    Pentagram, USA, 1992
    A hand-drawn cup of coffee extols the honest
    qualities of this traditional diner in New York.

1.

2.

3.

4.

5.

6.

7.

8.

9.

10.

11.

1. **Soroush Publications** publishing, Iran
   Ghobad Shiva, Iran, 1971
   Three simple shapes combine to define a row
   of books.
2. **Get London Reading** charity, UK
   KentLyons, UK, 2008
   A simple but effective image communicates the
   aim of this campaign.
3. **Salt Lake City Public Library** libraries, USA
   Pentagram, USA, 2001–03
   A simple, iconic symbol suggesting a shelf
   of books.
4. **Chicago Sun Times Books** publishing, USA
   Essex Two, USA, 1992
   A simple bibliophilic symbol for a publisher of
   periodicals, supplements and books.

5. **University of Wisconsin Extension
   Services** education, USA
   *John Rieben/University of Wisconsin–Madison
   Department of Art, USA, 2005*
   Two buildings suggest the form of an open book;
   symbol for an off-campus study programme.
6. **Denver Public Library** libraries, USA
   Unimark International, USA, c.1970s
   A dynamic abstract mark drawing inspiration
   from the shape of an open book.
7. **Mondi** paper, USA
   Unimark International, USA, c.1970s
   Two rolls of paper connect to form a simple but
   evocative mark.
8. **University of Eastern Finland** education, Finland
   Hahmo, Finland, 2008
   Simple graphic forms combine to create a person
   reading a book, suggesting learning and personal
   growth.

9. **Communist Party Publishing House**
   publishing, Bulgaria
   Stefan Kanchev, Bulgaria, c.1960s–70s
   A socialist star surrounded by open books.
10. **Fox River Paper** paper, USA
    Pentagram, USA, 1988
    The pages of an open book and a fox's face are
    combined in a memorable symbol.
11. **Athenæum** hospitality, UK
    FOUR IV, UK, 2006
    A hand-drawn book recalls the ancient Greek
    origin of the name of the company: *athenæum*
    suggests libraries and learning.

12.

12. Barron's publishing, USA
Milton Glaser, USA, 1980
A simple, elegant symbol by a true icon of
American graphic design.

13. Osterville Village Library libraries, USA
Danne Design, USA, 2006
An open book for a fundraising campaign to build
a new library in this historic Massachusetts town.

14. Library of Congress libraries, USA
Chermayeff & Geismar, USA, 2008
Symbol communicating both the essence of a
book and the American flag to represent the
national library.

15. Pantone colour systems, USA
Pentagram, UK, 2000
Part of a comprehensive rebrand, the new
symbol for Pantone recalls its well-known
colour-matching 'chips'.

16. Yellow Tent education, USA
Automatic Art and Design, USA, 2007
A mark symbolizing education and research
appeals to both adults and children. It was
designed for an educational and social think
tank in Portland, Oregon.

17. Persimmon Books publishing, UK
Pentagram, UK, 1989
A hand-drawn symbol suggesting the literary
fruit offered by this particular persimmon tree.

18. New Leaf Paper paper, USA
Elixir Design, USA, 1998
A graphic take on the phrase 'turning over a new
leaf' communicates the spirit of an environmentally
responsible paper manufacturer.

13.

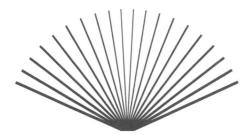

14.

15.

16.

17.

18.

1.

2.

3.

4.

5.

6.

1. **Booktailor** publishing, UK
   Thomas Manss & Company, Germany, 2000
   Symbol for a promotional Valentine's Day
   campaign for a publisher of customized
   travel guides.

2. **Gamida For Life** healthcare, Israel
   Dan Reisinger, Israel, 2000
   A distinctive heart symbol for a group
   of healthcare companies.

3. **Swiss Benevolent Society San Francisco**
   charity, USA
   Studio AND, USA/Switzerland, 2006
   A graphic reference to nationality and charity in
   this symbol for an organization set up in 1886 to
   assist Swiss immigrants.

4. **Cable Health Network** broadcasting, USA
   Chermayeff & Geismar, USA, 1982
   A playful symbol for a Viacom network
   broadcasting programmes dealing with physical
   and mental health.

5. **Instytut Matki i Dziecka** education, Poland
   Karol Sliwka, Poland, 1980
   A wholesome image conveys the idea of nurturing
   for a Polish parenting institute.

6. **Heart Foundation** healthcare, Australia
   Sadgrove Design, Australia, c.1980
   A simple heart motif is brought to life by a flaming
   torch, a symbol of light and hope.

7.

8.

9.

10.

11.

12.

7. **Habitat** retail, UK
    Graphic Thought Facility, UK, 2002
    Home is where the heart is; an elegant symbol for a leading high-street furnishing retailer.

8. **Coastal Thoracic Surgical Associates**
    healthcare, USA
    Morvil Advertising + Design Group, USA, 2007
    Clarity of communication prevails. A distinctive image of lungs indicates the surgical specialism.

9. **Agnette Bakery** food and beverages, Japan
    Stockholm Design Lab, Sweden, 2005
    A pretzel-shaped heart conveys a passion for baking in this symbol for a Japanese chain with over 450 bakery shops.

10. **Lifemark** healthcare, USA
    Pentagram, USA, 1999
    An organization providing services to chronically ill populations.

11. **Lenox Hill Heart and Vascular Institute of New York** healthcare, USA
    Arnold Saks Associates, USA, 1998
    An elegant, symmetrical mark identifies both the heart and lungs.

12. **College Town** clothing and accessories, USA
    BrandEquity, USA, 1972
    This symbol for a manufacturer of women's clothing identifies its parent brand with an overtly positive tone.

13.

14.

15.

16.

17.

18.

19.

20.

21.

22.

13. Unilever Heartmarque food and beverages, UK
Carter Wong Design, UK, 1996
Moving away from sun, sea and sand, this mark for Unilever's ice-cream business supported a new, more emotive proposition of 'natural togetherness'.

14. Showa textiles, Japan
Katsuichi Ito Design Office, Japan, 1989
Resembling a roll of fabric, this symbol expresses a passionate, hands-on approach to textile manufacturing.

15. Albalact food and beverages, Romania
Brandient, Romania, 2005
A distinctly modern mark combines a healthy heart with udders to express the brand's products.

16. Europharm pharmaceuticals, UK
Brandient, Romania, 2003
Following a takeover by GlaxoSmithKline, this refreshed mark retains the serpent and heart motifs to support the proposition 'tradition and change, wholeheartedly'.

17. Comfortet Inc. clothing and accessories, USA
Essex Two, USA, 1999
A warm, health-orientated symbol for a brand of bras and undergarments designed for clinical and athletic needs.

18. Felt charity, UK
Funnel Creative, UK, 2005
A floral symbol comprising four hearts was designed for a 'legacies in wills' initiative started by four UK charities.

19. Kere Kere restaurants, Australia
Studio Pip and Co., Australia, 2009
The symbol for a university café reflects the name: *kerekere* is the Fijian custom of giving without expecting repayment.

20. The Art Fund arts and culture/charity, UK
johnson banks, UK, 2005
This symbol is part of an identity fusing love and art for a charity focused on stopping works of art from leaving the UK.

21. CFDA professional associations, USA
Arnell, USA, 2001
A playful mark conveys the passion, nationality and industry of the Council of Fashion Designers of America.

22. Shahal Telemedicine healthcare, Israel
Danny Goldberg Design, Israel, 2005
A natural heart motif for Israel's leading specialist in advanced telemedicine services.

KLM

Transport, The Netherlands
F. H. K. Henrion, UK, 1961

Founded in 1919, Royal Dutch Airlines – or Koninklijke Luchtvaart Maatschappij (literally 'Royal Aviation Company') – is the oldest carrier in the world still operating under its original name. Designed by F. H. K. Henrion (1914–90), KLM's stylized crown symbol has a few years on the clock as well – not that you can tell.

Born in Nuremberg, Germany, Henrion moved to England in 1936 where, following a short period in internment, he worked for the Ministry of Information designing posters for initiatives such as the famous Dig For Victory campaign during the Second World War. A pioneer in the emerging field of corporate identity, his clients included the Post Office, British European Airways and the National Theatre. Henrion was widely fêted for his achievements – a Royal Designer for Industry and an early member of Alliance Graphique Internationale (AGI), he was awarded both the MBE (in 1951) and the OBE (in 1985).

His reputation was already established when he designed KLM's identity in 1961, but it didn't stop the Dutch airline questioning his design. Apparently, KLM accepted the design only after protracted deliberation, considering it too advanced. It is perhaps a testament to KLM's vision and courage that the symbol entered service at all, but the fact that it is still in use today – even following KLM's merger with Air France in 2004 (to form Air France-KLM) – is testament to Henrion's simple, bold and undeniably modern design.

The KLM logo always comprises both the crown symbol and the KLM name: they are only ever used in application together. We are grateful to the KLM for making an exception on this occasion.

1.

2.

3.

4.

5.

6.

7.

8.

9.

1. **Royal Wegener** publishing, The Netherlands
Edenspiekermann, The Netherlands, 2003
A distinctly modern symbol reflecting the regal name and heritage of one of Holland's largest publishers.

2. **Asaris Cosmetic** health and beauty, Switzerland
Karol Sliwka, Poland, 1988
A stylized crown resembling a patch of flowers suggests an aspirational tone and natural beauty.

3. **Sanssouci Film GmbH** film, Germany
Filmgraphik, Germany, 2003
Symbol for a film and TV production company.

4. **TNT Post** postal services, The Netherlands
Studio Dumbar, The Netherlands, 2006
A simple illustration conveys a modern spirit while reflecting the heritage of the Royal TNT Post brand.

5. **KPN** broadcasting/telecoms, The Netherlands
Studio Dumbar, The Netherlands, 2006
A strong, creative symbol referencing the heritage of Holland's leading telecom, Internet and television company.

6. **The Royal Theatre** arts and culture, Denmark
e-Types, Denmark, 2005
A stylized crown conveys heritage and royal patronage.

10.

11.

7. **Bakoma SA** food and beverages, Poland
    Karol Sliwka, Poland, 1989
    Mark reflecting a leading Polish dairy brand's
    commitment to nature.

8. **Crown CRO** healthcare, Finland
    Porkka & Kuutsa, Finland, 2008
    A splash of water creates both a crown and
    interacting figures in this symbol for a partner
    company conducting clinical trials in Nordic and
    Baltic countries.

9. **Wasa** food and beverages, Sweden
    Carter Wong Design, UK, 2001
    Crowns are ubiquitous in Sweden, portraying
    heritage or royal patronage; this symbol for a
    wheat-bread brand makes the crown ownable
    by basing it on a wheatsheaf.

10. **The Royal Parks** public space, UK
    Moon Brand, UK, 1993
    A crown of leaves meets with royal approval; the
    wood engraved quality of the white lines on black
    lends the symbol an appropriately warm and
    wholesome personality.

11. **The New York Palace** hospitality, USA
    & SMITH, UK, 2008
    A distinctly regal mark reflecting the timeless
    elegance of one of Manhattan's truly iconic
    hotels; The New York Palace is a Dorchester
    Collection hotel.

1.

2.

3.

4.

5.

6.

7.

8.

9.

10.

11.

12.

13.

1. **Gemeinde Köniz** regional identity, Switzerland
   Atelier Bundi, Switzerland, 1991
   A modern reworking of the region's traditional
   crest suggests both heritage and progress.
2. **Ballerup Kommune** municipality, Denmark
   Bysted, Denmark, 2007
   Symbol for a town situated in the north-western
   suburb of Copenhagen; one of several marks
   designed by Bysted following a programme of
   municipal reform.
3. **DIF** finance, The Netherlands
   Studio Bau Winkel, The Netherlands, 2005
   Symbol for the Dutch Infrastructure Fund,
   designed to present a powerful, competitive
   image.
4. **Isala Klinieken Zwolle** healthcare,
   The Netherlands
   Studio Bau Winkel, The Netherlands, 2001
   Symbol for a leading healthcare group based in
   Zwolle; inspired by the nearby River Ijssel (Isala).

5. **Korea Sparkling** tourism, South Korea
   Interbrand, international, 2007
   Symbol embodying the vitality and enthusiasm
   of South Korea; it evokes the powerful emotions
   and dynamism of local culture.
6. **Symbion Health** healthcare, Australia
   Cato Partners, Australia, 2006
   Mark symbolizing the continuity of life and the
   core brand values of transparency, openness and
   future growth.
7. **Favrskov Kommune** municipality, Denmark
   Bysted, Denmark, 2006
   Symbol for a municipality in the Central Jutland
   Region; one of several marks designed by Bysted
   following a programme of municipal reform.
8. **Sentiel** retail, UK
   Ivalyo Nikolov, Bulgaria, 2004
   The shield and fountain-pen motif suggests
   intelligence and heritage.
9. **Harvard Pilgrim Health Care** healthcare, USA
   BrandEquity, USA, 1995
   A new name and symbol for two merged
   companies; the mark is a refined version of an
   existing logo belonging to one of the companies.

10. **CEC Bank** finance, Romania
    Brandient, Romania, 2003
    The oak leaf is a Romanian symbol of honesty,
    longevity and stability, and the shield implies
    security.
11. **Inertia** music, Australia
    Mark Gowing, Australia, 2008
    Symbol for an independent record label known
    for signing high-quality, creative and forward-
    thinking musicians from Australia and overseas.
12. **Greve Kommune** municipality, Denmark
    Bysted, Denmark, 2006
    Symbol for a municipality located south-west of
    Copenhagen; one of several marks designed by
    Bysted following a programme of municipal
    reform.
13. **NHH** education, Norway
    Mission Design, Norway, 2006
    A heraldic symbol that respects a proud heritage
    while providing one of Europe's leading business
    schools with a fresh, up-to-date image.

14.

15.

16.

17.

14. Rudersdal Kommune municipality, Denmark
Bysted, Denmark, 2006
Symbol for a municipality north of Copenhagen;
one of several marks designed by Bysted
following a programme of municipal reform.

15. St. Vincent Catholic Medical Centers
healthcare, USA
Doyle Partners, USA, 1995
This symbol is part of an identity marking the
merger of eight of New York City's Catholic
hospitals. It conveys modern healthcare
with strong Catholic traditions.

16. Haderslev Kommune municipality, Denmark
Bysted, Denmark, 2006
Symbol for a municipality in southern Denmark;
one of several marks designed by Bysted
following a programme of municipal reform.

17. Faaborg-Midtfyn municipality, Denmark
Bysted, Denmark, 2006
Symbol for a municipality in southern Denmark;
one of several marks designed by Bysted
following a programme of municipal reform.

18. Danmark Post postal services, Denmark
Kontrapunkt, Denmark, 1994
Symbol signalling an efficient, modern business,
supported by a proud nod to both tradition and
heritage.

19. The Danish Police public services, Denmark
e-Types, Denmark, 2003
A modernized heraldic device suggests both
integrity and heritage.

18.

10.

1.

2.

3.

4.

5.

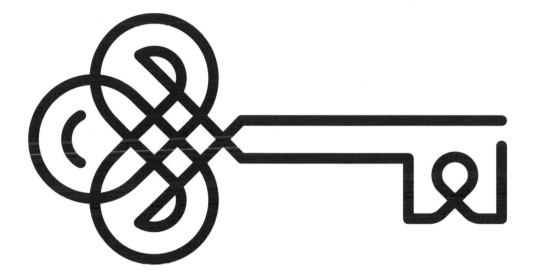

1. **Offenhaltenduerfen.at** legislative campaigns,
   Austria
   Buero X Vienna, Austria, 2007
   The shopping bag and open padlock motif
   expresses the organization's aim to liberalize
   opening hours in Vienna.
2. **Hemasafe** healthcare, USA
   Pentagram, USA, 1995
   This simple mark for a blood-bank franchise
   combines notions of security with a heart motif.

3. **Royal Key** retail, USA
   Ivalyo Nikolov, Bulgaria, 2005
   A key on a shield illustrates the company name in
   a suitably regal tone.
4. **Center for Architecture** arts and culture, USA
   Pentagram, USA, 2001
   Public centre dedicated to New York and the
   built environment.

5. **Neon Birdcage** events, UK
   Magpie Studio, UK, 2009
   Avoiding cliché, the symbol for this boutique
   events platform employs a key symbol, suggesting
   a way to unlock the cage, and the insights and
   knowledge within it.

CLIENT INDEX

DESIGNER INDEX

Where a designer appears more than once on the same page, the number of instances is given in brackets.

SECTOR INDEX

PICTURE CREDITS

Apple
Pages 178–179: Apple and the Apple logo are trademarks of Apple Inc., registered in the U.S. and other countries. Images courtesy of Apple

BOAC
Pages 212–213: Speedbird symbol and images courtesy of the British Airways Heritage collection

British Rail
Page 138: The British Rail logo is a registered trade mark in the name of the Secretary of State for the Department for Transport
Page 139 bottom left: Image courtesy of transportlibrary.com / Photography by Paul Childs
Page 139 bottom right: 'National Railway Museum/SSPL'

CBS
(Columbia Broadcasting System)
Pages 254–257: Images and logo courtesy of CBS

Centre Georges Pompidou
Pages 274–277 © Centre Pompidou. Architects: Renzo Piano and Richard Rogers
Page 275: Photo Georges Meguerditchian
Pages 276–277: Print applications designed by Christian Beneyton

CND
Page 31: Image © Keystone PA Ltd

Continental Airlines
Page 100: Logo courtesy of Continental Airlines;
Pages 101–103: Images courtesy of the Saul Bass Estate and of the Academy of Motion Picture Arts and Sciences

Deutsche Bank
Pages 34–35: Logo and images courtesy of Deutsche Bank

KLM
Pages 304–305 logo and image © KLM

MOT
Page 42: Logo courtesy of VOSA

Munich Olympics 1972
Pages 112–113: Logo and poster © IOC (International Olympic Committee)

New York Public Library
(NYPL)
Page 195: Drawings by Marc Blaustein
Page 196: Design, video stills: Marc Blaustein
Page 197: Design, tote bag: Matthew Poor, Marc Blaustein

Nike
Pages 106–107: Nike Swoosh logo and images courtesy of Nike INC

Nouveau Théâtre de Montreuil
Page 269: Image of Building – Architects: Dominique Coulon & Associés; Photo: Jean-Marie Monthiers

Shell
Pages 218–219: © Shell International Limited

Sprint
Page 201: Phone image © David Arky Photography

Swiss Federal Railway
(SBB CFF FFS)
Pages 132–133: © SBB

TfL
Page 20–21: Roundels reproduced by kind permission of Transport for London © ®;
Page 22: Photos courtesy of transportlibrary.com, photography by Paul Childs;
Page 23: London Transport by Man Ray © TfL from the London Transport Museum Collection

WWF
Page 186: © 1986 Panda Symbol WWF – World Wide Fund For Nature (Formerly World Wildlife Fund) ® 'WWF' is a WWF Registered Trademark.
Page 187 top: © Jürgen Freund / WWF-Canon
Page 187 bottom: © Martin Harvey / WWF-Canon
Page 188 top left: © Jürgen Freund / WWF-Canon
Page 188 top right: © Edward Parker / WWF-Canon
Page 188 bottom: © WWF-Canon / Simon Rawles
Page 189 top: © WWF-Canon / Richard Stonehouse
Page 189 bottom: © Slawek Jankowski / WWF

Acknowledgements

We extend our gratitude to all the designers, archivists, marketing managers, publishers, PR officers and image researchers without whose time and benevolence this project would not have been possible.

In particular, we would like to thank: Kevin Rau, Creative Director at rauhaus design, for providing access to work by the legendary Unimark International; John Rieben; Bill Bogusky of The Brothers Bogusky; R. Roger Remington; Ken and Denis Parkhurst; Howard York of York Branding; Paul Farber, editor of *The Journal of the History of Biology* (and Ties Nijssen at the journal's publisher, Springer); Jennifer Bass, daughter of the late Saul Bass; Ruther Eksell, wife of the late Olle Eksell, and Britt Eksell; Pat Schleger, wife of the late Hans Schleger; Lucy Clark at Lund Humphries; Simon Beresford-Smith at Pentagram; David Pearce at Akitt, Swanson and Pearce Architects Inc.; Tina Dakin at CBS; Magdalina Stancheva and the family of Stefan Kanchev; Ben Soffa and everybody at CND; Marie Damsgaard at Mærsk; Stella Warmuth at Lufthansa; Jon Jeffery at Bibliothèque; Jason Woolf and Hannes Rupprecht, project managers for design and branding at Shell International Limited; Saskia Boersma at Transport for London; Tony Howard; Jo Lightfoot and Susie May at Laurence King; everybody at &SMITH Design; and picture researcher Ida Riveros, whose contribution was invaluable.

Steven Bateman would also like to thank Rachel for her love, patience and support.